ORTHO'S All About

Sprinklers
and Drip Systems

Meredith® Books
Des Moines, Iowa

Ortho® Books
An imprint of Meredith® Books

Ortho's All About Sprinklers and Drip Systems
Solaris Book Development Team
Publisher: Robert B. Loperena
Editorial Director: Christine Jordan
Managing Editor: Sally W. Smith
Acquisitions Editors: Robert J. Beckstrom,
    Michael D. Smith
Publisher's Assistant: Joni Christiansen
Graphics Coordinator: Sally J. French
Editorial Coordinator: Cass Dempsey
Copyeditor: Melinda Levine
Proofreader: Alice Mace Nakanishi
Project Editor: Karen K. Johnson
Writer: Larry Hodgson
Illustrator: Tony Davis
Principal Photographer: Michael Landis

Meredith Book Development Team
Editor: Ben Allen
Art Director: Tom Wegner
Contributing Copy Editor: Barbara Feller-Roth
Contributing Proofreader: Carol Turner
Electronic Production Coordinator: Paula Forest
Editorial Assistant: Kathy Stevens
Production Director: Douglas M. Johnston
Production Manager: Pam Kvitne
Assistant Prepress Coordinator: Marjorie J. Schenkelberg

**Additional Editorial Contributions from
    Greenleaf Publishing**
Publishing Director: Dave Toht
Associate Editor: Steve Cory
Assistant Editor: Rebecca JonMichaels
Editorial Art Director: Jean DeVaty
Design: Melanie Lawson Design
Illustrations: Tony Davis
Additional Photography: Dan Stultz
Technical Consultant: Michael Clark

Meredith® Books
Editor in Chief: James D. Blume
Managing Editor: Gregory H. Kayko

Director, Sales & Marketing, Retail: Michael A. Peterson
Director, Sales & Marketing, Special Markets:
    Rita McMullen
Director, Sales & Marketing, Home & Garden Center
    Channel: Ray Wolf
Director, Operations: Valerie Wiese

Vice President, General Manager: Jamie L. Martin

Meredith Publishing Group
President, Publishing Group: Christopher M. Little
Vice President, Consumer Marketing & Development:
    Hal Oringer

Meredith Corporation
Chairman and Chief Executive Officer: William T. Kerr
Chairman of the Executive Committee: E.T. Meredith III

Thanks to
Autumn Skies Landscapes
Central Valley Builders Supply
Deborah Cowder
Malia Landis
David and Joy Long
Anthony Torres
The Urban Farmer Store
David Van Ness

Additional Photographers
Allen Boger: 87
Patricia Bruno/Positive Images: 6T
Gay Bumgarner, Photo/Nats: 20
Walter Chandoha: 78
Josephine Coatsworth: 18–19, 89T
Alan Copeland: 57
Crandall & Crandall: 36L, 38BL, 38T, 88
J. Eakes, Photo/Nats: 23B
Derek Fell: 11
David Goldberg: 80T
Saxon Holt: 8, 13, 17, 38BR, 62B
Jerry Howard/Positive Images: 14
Anita Sabarese: 39T

All of us at Ortho® Books are dedicated to providing you
with the information and ideas you need to enhance your
home and garden. We welcome your comments and
suggestions about this book. Write to us at:
Meredith Corporation
Ortho Books
1716 Locust St.
Des Moines, IA 50309–3023

If you would like more information on other Ortho
products, call 800-225-2883 or visit us at www.ortho.com

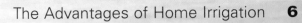

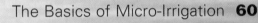

A properly planned irrigation system makes it easy to keep your landscape in tip-top shape.

THE BASICS OF HOME IRRIGATION

If you spend too much time watering, or if your lawn, garden, and shrubs sometimes get less water than they need, home irrigation may be the solution. Home irrigation systems are reliable and nearly invisible, and they often pay for themselves. But irrigation isn't for every yard or garden; read this chapter to decide if it's for yours.

Irrigation systems are cost-effective, unobtrusive, and durable. An automatic system will make your life a bit easier. A properly installed irrigation system will supply the correct amount of water to the intended place, so your plants and lawn will be thoroughly fed without wasting water.

When planning your system, consider not only your climate but also the microclimates on your property caused by varying amounts of shade and wind. Also, factor in the type of soil you have. Plan your landscaping along with your irrigation system for the best results over the long term.

THE ADVANTAGES OF HOME IRRIGATION

Landscaping not only beautifies your home, it also increases its value. Anything that helps you maintain your landscaping is worth considering. This means irrigation could be one of the best home investments you can make.

HEALTHY, GREEN GARDENS

There are no two ways about it: Plants grow best when all their watering needs are met in a timely manner. Haphazard, irregular watering results in patchy, uneven growth. Compare the yards in your neighborhood that are irrigated with those that are not. This shouldn't be hard; they can usually be distinguished from a distance. The irrigated lawns are generally greener and lusher. Their hedges, trees, and shrubs are denser and less subject to summer yellowing, and their flower gardens grow more quickly and remain in peak bloom longer. Vegetable gardens, especially, are much more productive, often yielding twice as much produce per square foot as do nonirrigated gardens, and the vegetables are often larger, better formed, tastier, and earlier to mature.

Proper irrigation also results in healthier plants. Plants that are watered irregularly develop smaller root systems, grow more slowly, and are more susceptible to insects, disease, and cold damage than those that receive even watering. Many insects are actually attracted to wilted, yellowing leaves. Irregular hose watering can splash leaves with contaminated soil, spreading many bacterial and fungal diseases. Properly planned irrigation can direct water at root level and can be timed to coincide with the drying effect of the sun, which can lessen disease spread.

Once installed, an irrigation system will blend in with the landscape and become nearly invisible.

Irregular watering leads to weak, patchy growth, increased insect problems, and yellowed leaves.

PRACTICALITY AND CONVENIENCE

Of course, you can water by hand and save the expense of irrigation, but are you always around at the right time? And do you always have the time? Running around the yard moving hoses and sprinklers is not always fun, and local restrictions that may limit watering to impossible hours of the night make hand watering even less appealing. That's why irrigation systems are so practical. With the use of a timer, it is possible to set the system to start when you are asleep or at work. You can even program your system to come on regularly while you are away on vacation.

EASY INSTALLATION: Any irrigation system is going to take some installation, but techniques have improved and been simplified greatly since home irrigation first became readily available after World War II. The old-fashioned metal-pipe systems were unwieldy and complicated to install and required soldering, specialized equipment, and considerable skill.

Modern irrigation systems make installation easy, with piping and heads that simply snap or glue together, and tubing that is easily cut to appropriate lengths. It is now not only feasible but relatively easy to install a modest system in a couple of weekends, especially if the irrigation plans have been carefully prepared. Most irrigation suppliers offer a wide range of products to meet almost every need.

You can also rent trenching equipment that makes the most laborious part of installation, digging the holes, almost easy. The equipment causes so little damage to the lawn and garden that, within only a week, you can barely see any evidence of the digging.

COST-EFFECTIVENESS: The major concern of any homeowner considering installing an irrigation system used to be the cost. The arrival of new lightweight materials has changed all that, bringing the cost of installing a system within the reach of just about every budget. Although prices vary widely according to the size of the property and its particular needs, many homeowners find an efficient irrigation system can usually be installed for less than $2,000 and often less than $1,000. Most systems will pay for themselves in only a few years through improved growth of lawn and garden, reduced loss of plants to drought, and greatly de-creased yard maintenance. Furthermore, irrigation increases the value of property; the presence of an effective irrigation system can make a major difference in its salability.

TAILOR-MADE: Lawn and garden irrigation can be tailored to your specific needs. Hose-driven sprinklers water everything haphazardly, overwatering slopes and leaving dry pockets behind shrubs and trees. Irrigation, on the other hand, can be extremely efficient. Different circuits with watering periods that vary in both frequency and duration ensure each planting gets the water it needs, when it needs it. And you can plan the system so it waters just the lawns and gardens, not the sidewalks, windows, and streets.

You can also match the level of control to your needs: An irrigation system can be almost entirely automated, or completely manual, or anywhere in between. Because landscape plantings grow and change over time, watering requirements will also change—and modern irrigation systems are easily adaptable. Sprayer heads can be adjusted or changed, and high-pressure systems using sprinklers and bubblers can be converted to low-pressure systems using drip irrigation or micro-sprinklers. It is also a relatively easy matter to add new sprayer heads to an existing system, as long as some space is left for future expansion during the initial planning.

NEARLY INVISIBLE: You can barely see a well-planned irrigation system—it is nearly invisible. Underground pipes and discreetly placed sprayers or drippers blend into the landscape. Some sprinklers even pop up to water, then disappear underground when their job is done. Compare that with the look of a hand-watered landscape: tangled hoses in dangerous array all over the yard.

BUILT TO LAST: Modern irrigation systems are composed mostly of weather-resistant plastic products, which are not subject to rust or decomposition. They can be expected to last 20 years or more, and some carry lifetime guarantees on product workmanship. Individual parts—such as sprinkler heads—that are exposed to damage from passing feet, flying footballs, and lawn mowers can easily be adjusted or replaced. In fact, the only routine maintenance needed in most climates is annual draining, occasional cleaning of exposed parts, and, in the case of drip systems, regular flushing to prevent the buildup of deposits. If even that small amount of maintenance sounds like too much, you can

Hand watering can be time-consuming, messy, and wastes water.

THE ADVANTAGES OF HOME IRRIGATION
continued

contract out the maintenance to a specialist for a modest fee.

LOW-MAINTENANCE GARDENING: As many homeowners do, you may dream of a beautiful landscape that takes care of itself. An irrigation system brings you several steps closer to this goal. If you are looking for maximum upkeep for minimal effort, you will want to automate the system to the utmost (see "Automatic Watering," page 80). The use of a water sensor or rain gauge, in addition to the basic timer, means the system will require the least possible human intervention. If you are looking for a less-automated system—perhaps because you are a weekend gardener and want a more hands-on approach—you might prefer an entirely manual system or a semiautomatic one (see "Using Your System," page 78).

With the proper irrigation system, your landscape will practically water itself, leaving you more time to appreciate it.

LOW-MAINTENANCE COVER-UPS:
Irrigation is well suited to a process that is central to low-maintenance gardening—mulching. By covering the surface of the soil, mulch prevents weed germination, keeps the ground cooler, slows down evaporation, and generally decreases yard upkeep. Mulch is also the perfect cover for the unattractive tubing of many drip systems.

Another low-maintenance cover-up for tubing is living ground cover, such as low-growing, leafy shrubs, vines, and perennials. These plants are used frequently in low-maintenance gardens, under trees, and on slopes to prevent erosion and provide a low-care substitute for heavy-upkeep lawns. Also, with adequate, regular irrigation, ground covers become established more rapidly and are healthier.

Other low-care plants, such as drought-tolerant trees, shrubs, and ornamental vines, combine perfectly with mulch and irrigation to create easy-care landscapes.

IRRIGATION AND CONSERVATION

Home irrigation not only provides a means of watering yards and gardens without carrying the hose from spot to spot and without getting wet, it also allows you to apply the appropriate amount of water at the best time, thereby conserving resources.

WATER, THE SOURCE OF PLANT LIFE

Water accounts for 60 to 90 percent of the weight of actively growing plants, including those growing in the desert. Plants use water to build leaves, flowers, and fruits; to transport minerals from the roots to the leaves; and to carry energy from the leaves to the roots—all the basic life processes. Plants are, however, wasteful of water. In nondesert plants, especially, most water is neither used for growth nor stored for future use but is given off in the form of water vapor through stomata, or breathing pores. Plants that do not receive adequate rainfall, therefore, quickly use up whatever water is available in the soil. This happens more rapidly under high heat, because plants transpire more quickly and thus lose water more rapidly.

When plants don't have enough water to carry on their normal life processes, their leaves lose their turgidity, and wilt. Wilted plants often recover if watered immediately, but some damage has generally been done. The fragile root hairs, through which plants absorb much of their water, must be in constant contact with at least a thin film of water or they will die. When a plant wilts aboveground, you can be sure root hairs are dying down below. Each time a plant wilts, more root hairs die, causing the plant's growth to slow down or stop.

Underwatered plants often lose part of their leaves, abort flower buds, or produce deformed, undersized fruits. Hand watering often puts plants through a constant cycle of drought and abundance that, at best, slows their growth and, at worst, can leave them weak and dying. Irrigation, on the other hand, supplies water just before the soil dries out. Properly irrigated plants never lack water and are healthier and more productive.

THE CORRECT AMOUNT OF WATER: Home irrigation uses piping to carry water from the main source of supply (the water main, a well, or a water tank) to the plants that need it. It can involve sprinklers and bubblers that operate under high pressure and visibly spray water onto plantings, often over long distances, or drip emitters that carry water under low pressure and deliver it to your plants drop by drop, practically unseen.

The principal goal of home irrigation is to water the root zones of plants, trees, and lawns in order to compensate for any moisture not provided by the environment. Irrigation is, therefore, most useful during periods of high heat and low rainfall. Not all plants require the same amount of water or the same frequency of irrigation (this is discussed in greater detail in the final chapter), but, in general, an irrigation system should keep all parts of the lawn and garden evenly moist throughout the growing season.

It is, however, important not to go overboard with irrigation. All plants need air at their roots. If the soil remains constantly waterlogged, any air present in the soil is used up and the roots can no longer breathe. As a result, the plant eventually rots and dies. It is essential that the soil remain slightly moist at all times or, if it is allowed to become saturated to the point of puddling, that the excess water be allowed to drain thoroughly before the next watering.

FERTILIZER NEEDS WATER: A proper water supply is vital to a plant's intake of minerals. Fertilizer is usually applied as a liquid or is watered in, because plants can absorb nutrients only when they are in liquid form. This explains why fertilizer and rich organic soils have so little effect on underwatered plants. The minerals are present, but the plants are unable to absorb them. In fact, fertilizing without supplying adequate water harms plants by causing root hairs to dry out.

ROOTS AND THE DRIP LINE: Because roots absorb almost all the water a plant requires (leaves absorb only small amounts), it is helpful to understand how they grow. Some roots, especially those of tall trees and desert shrubs, grow to great depths. The main job of these roots is to anchor the plants or to find water during extreme drought. Most other roots—including those most active in the absorption of water and minerals and in plant respiration—are within 2 feet of the surface of the soil.

Most root systems spread out horizontally a great distance from the stem of the plant. It used to be believed that the longest roots

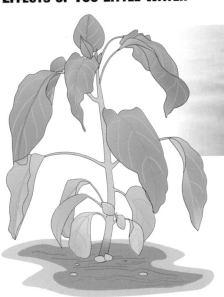

EFFECTS OF TOO LITTLE WATER

Wilted leaves are one sign that roots have been damaged by lack of water.

IRRIGATION AND CONSERVATION
continued

extended as far as the longest branch. An imaginary circle was drawn at this distance, and all watering was to be done within this drip line. It is now known that roots also extend well beyond the drip line. However, as you plot the watering needs of trees and shrubs, drawing a drip line is still a useful exercise, because most roots tend to be concentrated within a few feet on either side of the line.

WATER CONSERVATION

Home irrigation could appear wasteful, but it is actually less so than conventional watering. The average oscillating sprinkler loses almost as much of its moisture to the atmosphere as goes to water the garden. The droplets it shoots high into the air begin to

evaporate before reaching the plant. Water evaporates from the foliage before it sinks into the ground, especially in sunny or windy weather. Typically, too, a homeowner sets up a sprinkler and doesn't come back to turn it off until the ground is so saturated that water is running into the street. Also, because movable sprinklers are hard to adjust to the actual shapes of individual growing areas, water is wasted over patios and walkways.

High-pressure sprinkler irrigation is much more efficient (see "Sprinkler Irrigation," page 33). Designed to meet the needs of a specific yard, it sprays only lawns and gardens, not pavement. Irrigation segments are linked in circuits to supply water to plants with common needs. The water-hungry lawn can be moistened separately from a mass planting of drought-tolerant shrubs or deep-rooted trees. Slopes are notoriously hard to water. Most water simply runs off, leaving hillside

Sprinkler heads can be chosen or adjusted to spray odd-shaped areas of lawn without overspraying onto pavement.

Properly installed, a micro-sprinkler system is efficient and unobtrusive.

EXTENT OF ROOT SYSTEM

SIDE VIEW

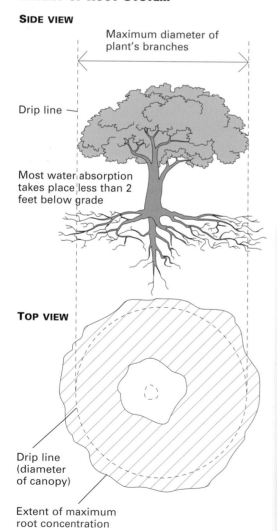

Maximum diameter of plant's branches

Drip line

Most water absorption takes place less than 2 feet below grade

TOP VIEW

Drip line (diameter of canopy)

Extent of maximum root concentration

Photo by Dan Stultz

A HISTORY OF IRRIGATION

Irrigation has been practiced for thousands of years. The first known traces of irrigation were found in Mesopotamia and date back to about 4000 B.C. These early efforts involved simple canals used to carry water to areas that didn't have enough. As time passed, irrigation techniques became more sophisticated. Using complicated systems of dikes and levees, plus human and animal power, the Mesopotamians carried water many miles from the nearest source and lifted it to great heights, enabling them to create the famous Hanging Gardens of Babylon, in about 600 B.C. By then, irrigation techniques had appeared in civilizations throughout the world, including Egypt, China, and Europe.

The Romans used pipes to carry water from one place to another; less water evaporates from pipes than from canals. Across the Mediterranean, the Sahara was already dotted with artificial oases supplied by irrigation. Irrigation also appeared simultaneously in the New World: Aztecan, Incan, and Mayan cultures all used it. In fact, much of the credit for their success can be traced to irrigation, which made it possible to produce the enormous quantities of food needed to support burgeoning populations.

Irrigation techniques have not always been limited to agricultural uses. Display gardens in Roman atria depended on water brought in from elsewhere, and estate gardens have long used irrigation. The use of sprinkler systems in home landscaping first became popular after World War II, and even drip irrigation, which sounded newfangled only a few years ago, has now become well established. The latest trend—and the thrust of this book—has been the development of user-friendly systems that anyone can install. You are not wandering blindfolded into unknown territory but, rather, are taking advantage of generations of technological advances.

This garden is reminiscent of the Hanging Gardens of Babylon, perhaps the most famous example of irrigation dating from ancient times.

plantings parched. By placing sloped areas on a separate system, it is possible to water them a little at a time, more frequently.

Low-pressure micro-irrigation is even more efficient (see "Micro-Irrigation," page 59). As water penetrates the soil drop by drop, often under a cover of protective mulch, almost no moisture is lost to direct evaporation. A micro-irrigation, or drip, system, as it is sometimes called, can be set up to deliver water exactly where it is needed—to the eager roots of vegetable plants, for example—while keeping the spaces between the rows so dry that weeds don't have a chance to sprout. Even individual flower pots on a patio can be watered while the surrounding wood deck or paving stones remain completely dry. With carefully planned drip irrigation, as much as 80 percent of the water goes to the plants rather than to the atmosphere. With conventional watering, that figure can be as low as 20 percent.

IRRIGATION AND LOCAL CONDITIONS

The homeowner struggling to maintain a green lawn in parched Arizona does not have the same needs as a backyard gardener in the cool and rainy Northwest. Here are guidelines for adapting irrigation to your specific requirements.

IRRIGATION FOR ALL CLIMATES

Irrigation systems are not just for hot, dry climates where lack of rain is a constant concern, but for all areas. Plants grow best when they receive adequate amounts of water throughout their growing season; even the short periods of drought that occur in otherwise moist climates can set back growth. Landscapes in moist climates, in fact, are often more seriously harmed by drought than are those in dry areas because plants in normally wet areas are not commonly selected because of their drought tolerance.

Most yards, regardless of the climate, have sections that receive less natural moisture than others. Areas such as slopes and spots under shallow-rooted trees or beneath roof overhangs may not receive much water and the plants there may suffer from drought stress. It is a rare yard that could not benefit from one form or another of irrigation.

WATERING RESTRICTIONS

In recent years, local watering restrictions have become commonplace. During the summer months, it is often no longer possible to water whenever you like; you have to heed the dictates of the municipality in which you live. Some municipalities limit the days that you may water; others specify the times of the day, usually late evening when industrial and domestic water use is at its lowest. During an extreme drought, watering may be prohibited for ornamental plants. Even under such restrictions, home irrigation allows you to make the maximum use of a limited resource.

When summer water restrictions are in effect, you can easily adjust the timing device to turn on the irrigation system at the time specified by municipal regulations. Under severe drought conditions, ornamentals that previously were properly irrigated have a greater chance of survival than do nonirrigated plants.

When watering ornamentals is prohibited, you'll usually still have the option to water food plants. If your vegetable garden is on a separate irrigation circuit, you can keep it going. Plants that have been watered correctly throughout their existence will have a healthy, extensive root system that will allow them to cope better with the stress of drought.

ANNUAL RAINFALL DISTRIBUTION

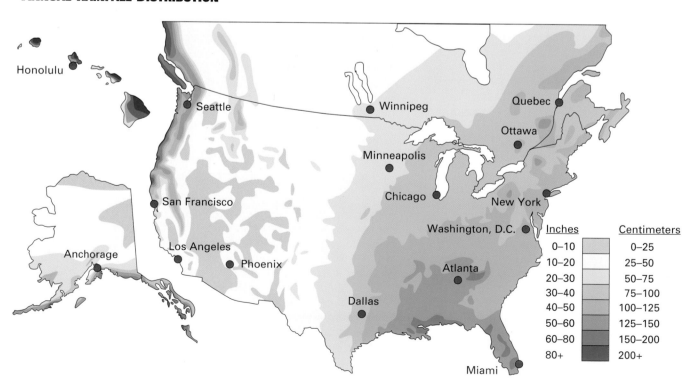

Inches		Centimeters
0–10		0–25
10–20		25–50
20–30		50–75
30–40		75–100
40–50		100–125
50–60		125–150
60–80		150–200
80+		200+

CLIMATE AND MICROCLIMATE

Irrigation requirements vary from region to region and season to season. In North America, irrigation needs are moderate in the Northeast and increase dramatically toward the Southwest. In areas with dusty, dry summer climates, such as Arizona and much of California, irrigation is not only recommended but is often essential to maintain any semblance of a green landscape.

Under arid conditions, installing lawn and garden irrigation is a matter of course when landscaping a yard or growing vegetables. Total annual rainfall, however, is not the only factor to consider. In the Pacific Northwest, for example, annual precipitation can reach 50 inches or more. The local vegetation is often referred to as rain forest, yet many areas experience severe and prolonged summer droughts. Precipitation is extremely heavy from fall through spring but much lighter during the summer. In other climates, notably in the Midwest and the East, average rainfall is relatively steady from month to month, but droughts are not infrequent, and several dry years in a row can play havoc with even well-established plantings. In these circumstances, an irrigation system can be beneficial.

Microclimate refers to very localized conditions—usually resulting from varying exposure to sun or protection from wind. You'll find that within your yard, there are different microclimates, areas that can be warmer or cooler, drier or more humid, than the rest of the landscape. Consider microclimates as you plan a system.

RAINFALL: You will need to watch out for the rain-shadow effect. This occurs in areas that are protected from the prevailing winds by structures or plantings and, therefore, don't receive as much moisture as other parts of the yard. They may need considerably more irrigation than do the areas more exposed to natural rainfall. Gardens under roof overhangs or covered walkways may be so dry they require an irrigation system even in an otherwise wet climate.

TEMPERATURE: The hotter the air, the faster water evaporates, and the sooner plants will need water again. Because temperatures in North America tend to be higher in southern areas, so are watering needs, even when the amount of rainfall is similar to that of a cooler climate. Likewise, when periods without rain do occur, they tend to cause less damage in northern climates where cool summers cause less evaporation.

This lush oasis may appear to be a water waster, but pinpoint irrigation and large shade trees ensure optimum use of a limited water supply.

IRRIGATION AND LOCAL CONDITIONS
continued

SOIL MOISTURE

EVENLY MOIST SOIL

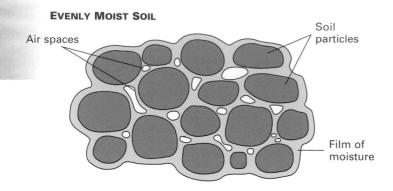

Air spaces

Soil particles

Film of moisture

WATERLOGGED SOIL

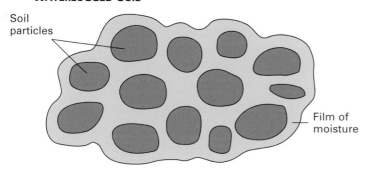

Soil particles

Film of moisture

Temperature variations can affect irrigation even within the average home landscape: Sunny lawns and beds are hotter than semishady or shady ones and lose more water to evaporation.

HUMIDITY: More water evaporates into dry air than into humid air, and air tends to be drier in the interior of the continent and more humid along the coast and near large bodies of water such as the Great Lakes. Homeowners in the interior of the continent will need to irrigate more than gardeners in coastal areas. Besides irrigating more frequently, gardeners in dry climates should consider using mulch around their plantings to reduce the evaporation rate.

WIND: Strong winds carry off moist air, causing plants to transpire more and lose moisture. Hedges, windbreaks, and plantings of shrubs and trees can reduce the influence of the wind and decrease irrigation needs, even in parts of the country where strong, dry winds are common. If parts of your garden are exposed to drying winds, plan to irrigate them on a separate circuit.

TYPES OF TOPSOIL

Soil type is often overlooked factor when planning home irrigation. You need to know what kind of topsoil you have. Natural soils are rarely composed of only one type of particle. Most are mixtures of varying amounts of clay, silt, sand, and humus, an organic material. Mixtures of different types of particles are called loam, and loam is further divided into sand, silt, and clay, depending on which soil type predominates.

In well-planned landscapes loam topsoil has been added to help absorb water and prevent the soil from becoming waterlogged by allowing surplus water to drain out quickly. Depending on whether the loam has the

Clay

Silt

Sand

Gravel

SOIL PARTICLES

Soil is composed of particles of various sizes; each type affects the drainage characteristics of the soil.

Type	Particle Size	Texture When Wet	Texture When Dry	Drainage	Notes
Clay	Very fine grained	Mucky and slippery. Can be kneaded in the hand like bread dough	Becomes compact and hard, like rock. Often cracks	Very poor to none	Clay actually absorbs water and minerals. It is hard to moisten, but when dampened it remains moist for a long time
Silt	Fine but larger grained than clay	Packs together well but can't be kneaded	Breaks up readily into a smooth, flourlike powder	Poor	Silt drains better than clay but not as well as sand
Sand	Large particles	Harsh and gritty to the touch. Doesn't hold together	Holds together poorly or not at all. Can't be squeezed	Water drains right through. Retains little moisture	Individual grains are visible to the naked eye
Gravel	Very large particles	Doesn't hold together	Doesn't hold together	Water drains right through. Dries out almost immediately	Individual particles can easily be picked up with the fingers

characteristics of sand or of clay, it will need either frequent or infrequent waterings.

CLAY LOAM: Plant roots often grow well in clay loam, but watering is difficult because water puddles up on the surface without sinking in. Most clay soils stay moist for long periods and need little irrigation or fertilization. Where clay loam predominates, pay careful attention to drainage. If water puddles in the area add plenty of organic matter to improve drainage.

SILT LOAM: A fairly fine-textured soil, silt loam may cause drainage problems if it tends to be more like clay than fine sand. It holds minerals and water well, and most plants thrive in it.

Building raised beds is an excellent way to overcome poor drainage and other soil problems.

IRRIGATION AND LOCAL CONDITIONS
continued

SANDY LOAM: Plant roots grow well in sandy loam, but watering is difficult, because the soil retains little moisture. There is no use watering sandy loam abundantly: Most of the water will simply drain away. If your soil is sandy, plan an irrigation system that can be turned on frequently but for shorter periods. Plants grown in sandy soils are more likely to suffer nutrient deficiencies, because minerals are easily washed out. The plants will therefore require light but frequent fertilizing.

GRAVEL: A few rocks in a garden do little harm, but if you find several pebbles in every handful of dirt, you will end up with bare patches or sparse yields. The only solution is to get rid of the rocks.

Loam is made up of a mixture of particles of sand, silt, and loam, plus organic materials.

nutrients and either so sandy that it drains too well or so rich in clay that it barely supports root growth. In some areas, the topsoil is directly on top of impervious rock or extremely compacted clay called hardpan. Whatever is under the topsoil will affect how frequently you should irrigate.

There is little reason to install irrigation in a yard that suffers major drainage problems. Why bring in more water if you're already having trouble getting rid of excess moisture? Put in drainage tiles, add high-quality topsoil, solidify slopes, and otherwise ensure excess water will drain quickly and safely before investing in irrigation.

SUBSOIL DRAINAGE

Having top-quality loam doesn't always guarantee good drainage. Most house lots are covered with a relatively thin layer of topsoil of moderate to good quality. Under this is a deep layer of subsoil that is generally low in

A SOIL DRAINAGE TEST

To get a better idea of the drainage capacity of the soil in your yard, choose a day when the soil is relatively dry, then dig a hole about a foot deep and a foot across. Pour in a bucket of water and watch the water in the hole.

■ If the water drains out almost as fast as you can pour it in, your subsoil is probably sandy and drains too well. You will need to irrigate frequently to keep the soil from drying out.

■ If the hole fills with water, then drains within a few minutes, you have good to fair drainage. Irrigation is especially easy and effective with such soils.

■ If the water is very slow to drain, you have poor drainage. Add drainage tiles before installing an irrigation system and improve the soil through soil amendments. If you are not ready for such large-scale modifications, consider raised beds filled with good topsoil for vegetable plots and small flower gardens.

SOIL DRAINAGE TEST

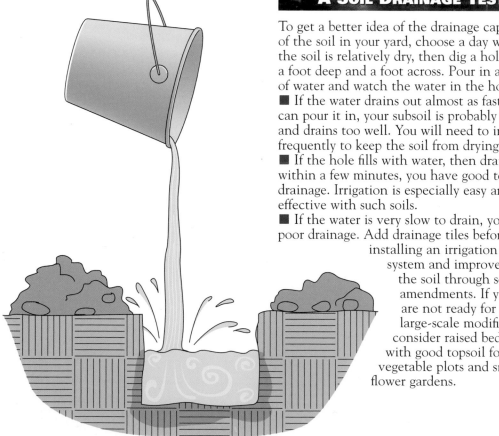

INVESTING IN IRRIGATION

Although irrigation makes landscape maintenance easier, irrigation will not pay for itself for a long time if your watering needs are only occasional.

IS IRRIGATION NECESSARY?

Just as swimming pools sell like hotcakes during a long, hot summer, irrigation systems arc often bought in a rush during a drought. Think back over the last few years. If watering has been a chore almost every summer, installing an irrigation system will be well worthwhile. If most summers in your area are relatively rainy, and you water only a few times in the average year, don't be swayed by one dry summer. Of course, even in a moist-summer climate, a few spots, such as under roof overhangs, do require constant attention. If you have such places consider a system for just those areas, rather than an all-encompassing one for the entire yard. A simple soaker hose, easily hidden with mulch and turned on manually, will only cost a few dollars yet will easily take care of an exceptionally dry bed in an otherwise humid climate.

Irrigation may not be a necessity if you actually enjoy hand watering and are generally available during the growing season. Just because your neighbors all have irrigation systems, you don't have to follow suit. Only you know whether the watering you have to carry out is an unbearably heavy chore or a pleasant interlude that keeps you active and in contact with the natural world.

THE RIGHT TIME

Consider irrigation only when a future landscape is mapped out on paper and the major infrastructures, such as retaining walls, are in place. Irrigation pipes, though solid, will not stand up to bulldozers, and sprinkler heads can be torn off during even minor landscaping projects.

The ideal moment for installing irrigation, if your budget allows it, is toward the end of your landscape project, when all infrastructures are in place, topsoil has been brought in and leveled out, trees and larger shrubs have been planted, and all that is left to do is to put in the perennials, lawns, and mulches. Irrigation piping will be easy to install in the loose soil and will be quickly hidden from sight by the final plantings.

XERISCAPING

You might want to plan the landscape to avoid needing irrigation. Xeriscaping, landscaping using drought-tolerant plants and water-conserving techniques, is practical in just about every climate. You can use well-spaced, deep-rooted trees, shrubs, ornamental grasses, and perennials in your landscape and mulch abundantly to save water. Ordinary lawn grasses requiring heavy watering can be passed over for more drought-tolerant varieties or for ground covers that require even less moisture. Plants well adapted to a Xeriscape vary from region to region. Check with your local extension service for suggestions of drought-tolerant plants suited to your area.

Even drought-tolerant plants require some watering, especially during the first year or two of growth. And, of course, in an otherwise Xeriscaped yard, you might want to reserve the luxury of a few lush, green oases maintained by irrigation.

Most people will find that irrigation of some form will be useful in at least parts of their yards. Once you have determined your general needs, you'll be ready for the next chapter, "Getting Started."

Irrigating a difficult corner, such as a flower bed under eaves, can be as simple as laying a length of porous, or soaker, hose.

*Proper planning is the secret to success with
any home-irrigation system.*

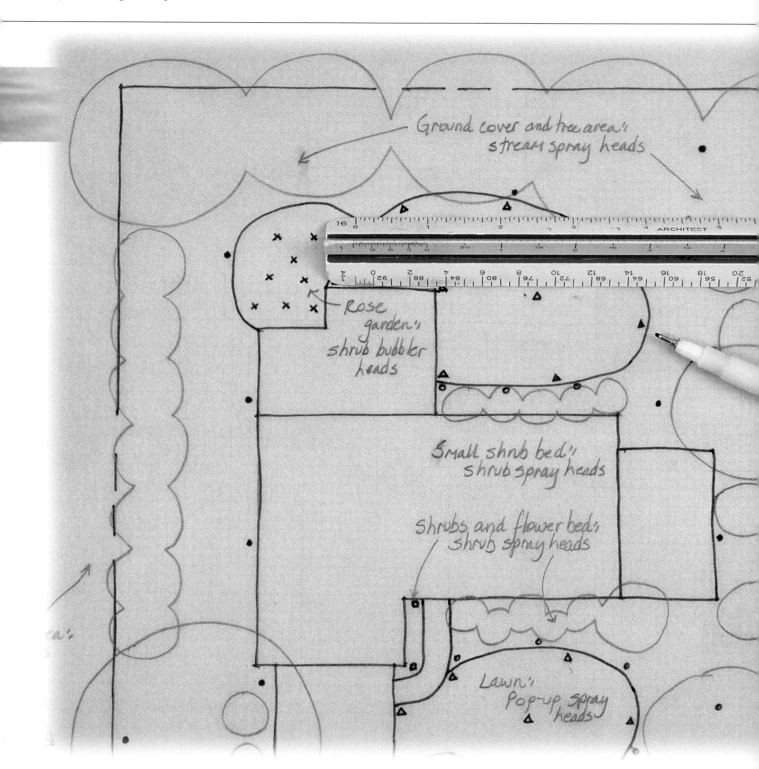

Ground cover and tree area's
stream spray heads

Rose garden's
shrub bubbler
heads

Small shrub bed's
shrub spray heads

Shrubs and flower bed's
shrub spray heads

Lawn's
Pop-up spray
heads

GETTING STARTED

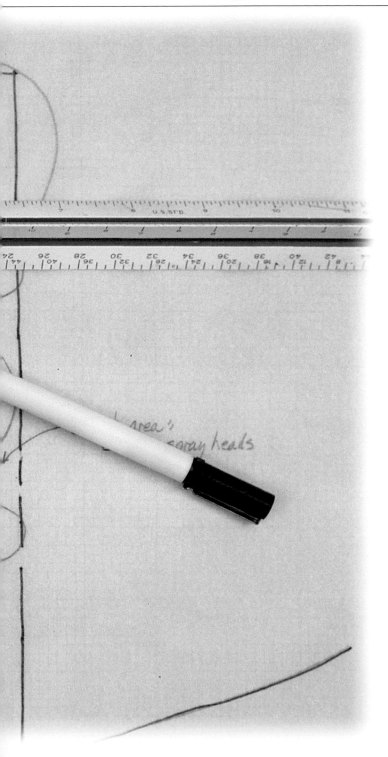

Before shopping for your irrigation system, you have a good deal of homework to do. Take a serious look at your yard, its needs, and your budget. Confirm the water capacity of your home and any municipal water restrictions. Draw up a detailed plan of the lot showing any factors that will affect the irrigation system. If you have any doubts or areas of confusion, consult a professional. It's far better to uncover a mistake at the planning stage than to discover a major flaw after the system is installed.

Remember, too, it is premature to install an irrigation system until you know all the details of the landscaping project. Whether you are moving into a new home or planning to change your yard, wait until the landscape plan is completed on paper before considering irrigation. Once this is done, you have a basic decision to make: Do you want a sprinkler system or a micro-irrigation system? Both have their advantages, so before preceding you'll need to consider all the factors discussed in this chapter.

TWO IMPORTANT QUESTIONS

Before you begin to draw up plans for an irrigation system, you'll first have to resolve two questions: Can I do the work myself or should I hire a professional? Should I use sprinkler irrigation or micro-irrigation? This section will help you make up your mind.

DO IT YOURSELF OR HIRE A PROFESSIONAL?

A pipe-puller can install poly or PVC pipe (shown here) quickly with little mess. It is best adapted to large, flat lawn areas.

Do-it-yourself irrigation is becoming more and more feasible. In some parts of the country, homeowners install nearly 75 percent of all irrigation systems. Installing an irrigation system is well within the reach of a capable homeowner who plans thoroughly and works carefully. But digging trenches, installing piping, making connections, and carrying out verifications constitute a lengthy process. Allow several weekends to get the entire system up and running.

All this work does require physical effort, but isn't backbreaking so long as you work carefully. You need little in the way of specialized equipment, and what you do need you can often rent. Doing the job yourself usually costs about two-thirds to one-half as much as having the system professionally installed. However, a poorly installed system could require extensive revisions diminishing any savings you derived from doing the job yourself. At certain steps in the process, you may be able to hire professional help without incurring major expense.

PLANNING AIDS: To avoid the most costly errors, you may want to consult a professional irrigator during the planning stage. Exact spray patterns are hard to plot and professionals are aware of specialized sprinklers and emitters for specific needs. In addition, irrigation systems are being constantly improved and updated. Without consulting an expert, you may have difficulty finding the most appropriate materials for your situation. Professional help is especially useful if your property has special needs or unusual conditions, such as extreme slopes or poor drainage.

Consult with people who specialize in irrigation systems. Salespeople at home centers or hardware stores may know less than they think they know. Consulting need not be expensive. Many dealers will draw a plan without charge if you buy the parts from them. Others charge a small fee, but you may find the advice is worth the expense. Follow the instructions in this chapter to gather the proper information and to draw an accurate plot of your lot, then take the plan to a dealer. The dealer will indicate the installations you need and supply a complete list of parts. If no dealers in your area offer such a service, look for companies that offer free computer-generated planning by mail. Obtain a form from a participating local dealer (a hardware store, garden center, or other store carrying irrigation equipment), plot your plan on the graph paper provided, answer the appropriate questions, and mail in the form. Your plan will soon be on its way.

TRENCHING FOR PIPES: You might also consider professional help when installing the piping. Digging shallow trenches is, of course, well within the capacity of most homeowners, but it is time-consuming and messy. A professional using trench-digging equipment can do the job more easily and quickly and the cost may not be prohibitive. Trenching equipment is most useful on large, open, flat areas. It is of little advantage in small yards with lots of corners to turn, in larger yards with raised beds, terracing, trees, and other obstacles, or on slopes. Trenching machines, especially tractor-driven ones, need a considerable amount of space in which to maneuver, and running them on anything other than large, flat areas or minor slopes can be dangerous.

If you decide to use trenching equipment, you can choose among several types of digging machines. The most basic is the sod remover, which carefully cuts out a narrow strip of sod you can put safely to one side. Then you can dig the trench by hand or use a trencher. Trenchers, as their name suggests, dig narrow trenches in the soil for both rigid PVC and flexible polyethylene (poly) piping. If you choose to use flexible poly pipe and if your soil is easily workable and not too rocky, you can hire a professional trencher who uses a pipe-pulling machine. This apparatus cuts a narrow slit in the lawn and then pulls the pipe through the ground, leaving the pipe ends exposed so you can add connections. The damage to the lawn is so minor that it heals in a few days.

PROBLEM AREAS: In a few situations, it is best to leave the installation work entirely to professionals. If you have severe erosion problems, very rocky soils, steep slopes, and delicate plantings that need protection you may want to hire a professional installer. One of the advantages of consulting a professional at the planning stage is learning whether you have any problem areas.

PLUMBING: You may not have the option of installing the pipe leading to your irrigation system yourself. Many municipalities require a licensed plumber install the copper pipe from the city main to the backflow preventer (the beginning of the irrigation system). If this is the case, you can still save money by preparing the work site beforehand. Determine the proper placement of the piping and backflow preventer, prepare any trenches or holes, and have all necessary parts on hand before the plumber gets there, so the job is strictly limited to installing and soldering pipes. If your municipality has no such restrictions, you can install the pipe and backflow preventer yourself. It is relatively easy to cut pipe and install a tee (see "Working with PVC Pipe", page 51).

LEARN ALL YOU CAN

Clinics and workshops provide a good introduction to irrigation. Many irrigation specialists offer them regularly, often free of charge. These clinics give you a chance to see how irrigation systems are planned and installed and to ask a few basic questions. Contact a dealer or a local horticultural society to find out about clinics and workshops in your area.

A trenching machine digs narrow trenches quickly.

STARTING SMALL

Irrigating your entire property can be a large undertaking, especially if you're doing all the planning and installation without the advice of a specialist. It can also be expensive. Consider irrigating just part of your property the first year. This will bring down the costs and give you a better idea about whether you feel at ease in the role of a do-it-yourself irrigator.

Choose a section with important watering needs yet without any special installation difficulties—a flat section of sunny lawn or a dry, sandy flower bed, for example. Then test the new system for a year, adapting it as necessary. By the following summer, you should have a better idea of how to proceed, what kind of system best suits your needs, and just how much of the installation you want to do on your own. If you plan for future additions from the start, there is no reason you can't build a complete irrigation system step-by-step over a number of years. While this approach may cost more in total, out-of-pocket costs may be more manageable.

SPRINKLER OR MICRO-IRRIGATION?

Probably no irrigation question is more confusing to the average homeowner than whether to install a high-pressure sprinkler system or a low-pressure micro-irrigation system. It is hard to determine which is the best overall, and the line between the two systems is quickly disappearing. You'll have to consider the advantages and disadvantages of each and decide which is best in your case.

SPRINKLER SYSTEMS: Sprinkler, or high-pressure, irrigation is by far the most common system in North America. When most people think of home irrigation, they think of a high-pressure sprinkler system. These systems use water piped under high pressure to spray the landscape.

Sprinkler systems are almost entirely underground. The sprinkler heads are the only visible components of a well-designed sprinkler system, and even these are generally

TWO IMPORTANT QUESTIONS
continued

unobtrusive or disappear underground when not in use. Because sprinkler systems require considerable trenching, they are usually more expensive than micro-irrigation systems. This isn't to say that micro-irrigation systems are simpler to install. The time required to assemble the large number of parts of a micro-irrigation system can be considerable. On the other hand, sprinkler systems normally require less upkeep than do micro-irrigation systems. Usually all they need are minor adjustments and annual drainage. As an investment, sprinkler systems may well be the best choice. Many prospective home buyers are leery of micro-irrigation, while believing sprinkler irrigation systems make landscape maintenance a snap.

Sprinkler systems use more water than micro-irrigation systems but less than conventional watering. Sprinkler systems are most appropriate where ease of care and landscape appearance are more important than water conservation. However, a properly installed sprinkler system is much less wasteful than one that is incorrectly installed. An overpressurized sprinkler system will produce a foglike spray, with a large percentage of the water blowing away. A correctly installed sprinkler system has just enough pressure to place water just where it is needed and will use water more efficiently.

Many homeowners find sprinkler systems most advantageous on large surfaces and lawns and less so in beds that are frequently dug up or changed, such as vegetable gardens. Rototillers can easily damage a sprinkler head or supply line. It is also difficult to adapt in-ground sprinkler systems to movable aboveground containers, such as hanging baskets and patio planters.

MICRO-IRRIGATION SYSTEMS: Micro-irrigation, or low-pressure, systems use little water at a time. Often, the spraying is not readily apparent. In many cases it is barely visible, even when the system is in full operation. Because water is applied at soil level, much less is lost to evaporation, making micro-irrigation an obvious choice in dry climates where water restrictions are severe.

Sprinkler systems are currently the most popular type of irrigation, especially where ease of care is more important than saving water.

Micro-irrigation can be concealed by burying service lines and covering emitters with mulch.

A well-planned micro-irrigation system leaves the soil surface relatively dry, but keeps the root zone constantly moist.

Until fairly recently, the most common form of micro-irrigation was drip irrigation. Now the most common form is a combination of drip and spray applications which are used as a surface system. The components of a micro-irrigation system are often partly hidden by decorative mulches. Because these tubes and emitters, run here and there through the garden, they are more visible than a sprinkler system. However, they have a number of advantages.

An emitter releases water drop by drop.

TWO IMPORTANT QUESTIONS
continued

TO DRIP OR TO SPRAY?

Which system—sprinkler or micro-irrigation—should you choose? Very possibly both, depending on your specific needs. This chart gives an idea of which system is most appropriate in which situations. If in doubt, consult an irrigation specialist.

	Sprinkler System	Micro-Irrigation System
Requires trenching	Yes	Sometimes
Water-saving capacity	Good	Excellent
Essentially invisible	Yes	Sometimes
Expensive to install	Yes	Sometimes
Limited maintenance requirements	Yes	Sometimes
Increases resale value of home	Yes	Sometimes
Additions easily made	Rarely	Often
Good for temporary use	No	Yes
Prevents weed germination	No	Under certain conditions
Helps prevent disease spread	Limited effect	Yes
Supplementary hand watering may be required	Rarely	Sometimes
Can be used on:		
Lawns	Yes	No*
Flower beds	Yes	Yes
Shrubs and trees	Yes	Yes
Vegetable gardens	Sometimes	Yes
Ground covers	Yes	Yes
Container plants	Sometimes	Yes
Slopes	Sometimes	Yes

ADVANTAGES OF MICRO-IRRIGATION

■ EASE OF INSTALLATION: Because digging is not necessary, drip irrigation is easy and inexpensive to install. Some hardware stores and garden centers carry inexpensive drip-irrigation kits that can be installed in a day. Because all parts of a drip system are easy to reach, the system is also highly adaptable: installing a new emitter may take seconds, whereas adding a new sprinkler head to a sprinkler system is a major undertaking. You can also pull up a drip-irrigation system in minutes if you need to till a bed or take in the system for the winter.

■ DURABILITY: In the past, breakdown was one of the major flaws of drip-irrigation systems. Emitters were far more likely to clog than were sprinklers, and changing emitters often became a regular and tedious chore.

Today, well-installed micro-irrigation systems are not as fragile as some people think. However, because of their more exposed parts, micro-irrigation systems are not quite as sturdy as sprinkler systems and need a little more care.

Micro-irrigation service lines can and probably should be buried. Much of the paraphernalia can be hidden under mulch and behind or under plantings. Simple micro-irrigation systems, such as porous hose, make inexpensive temporary fixes until you can afford or have time to install a more permanent solution.

■ DISEASE PREVENTION: Many plant diseases develop only when leaves are moist. With conventional watering and sprinkler irrigation, diseases are carried to susceptible leaves by drops of water bouncing from the soil. Bubbler heads, which water the ground more than they do the leaves, are often used in sprinkler irrigation when disease is a concern. Even with this precaution, sprinklers are more likely to spread disease than are micro-irrigation systems which do not even moisten the leaves.

■ WEED CONTROL: In climates with little or no summer rainfall, micro-irrigation can help prevent the spread of weeds. Since the surface of the soil remains dry, weed seeds can't germinate. You can keep surfaces such as the spaces between the rows in your vegetable garden or gravel walks and driveways almost entirely free of vegetation by not irrigating there at all. This is more difficult to accomplish with sprinkler irrigation, where wind-blown spray is much more likely to reach all parts of the yard. The disadvantage of this dry-surface effect is that desirable seed-grown plants won't grow. In a micro-irrigated vegetable garden, for example, you'll have to hand-water newly sown beds of carrots, lettuce, and corn until the roots of the young plants have reached into the moist soil below.

WHERE TO USE MICRO-IRRIGATION

Generally, micro-irrigation is most useful for small yards, vegetable beds, container gardens, and flower beds. You can even use it to water hanging baskets. It is also ideal for watering difficult spots, such as slopes where much of the water from sprinkler irrigation would otherwise simply run off. Until recently, micro-irrigation has not been considered adaptable to watering lawns, but new subsurface micro-irrigation systems designed specifically for that use are available.

A CLOSER LOOK AT YOUR PROPERTY

Each irrigation case is unique because each depends on a wide range of factors. In this section, you'll learn how to determine a vital element in planning your system—the water capacity of your home—as well as how to create a plan of your property.

MEASURING WATER CAPACITY

The first step in installing any irrigation system—particularly a sprinkler-type system—is determining the water capacity of your home. This is not hard to do. The four steps listed below and the charts on the following pages will help you.

1. CHECK WATER PRESSURE: The water pressure of a system varies according to how many water-using components are operating, the time of day (pressure is greater from late evening through early morning), and the weather conditions (lower pressure occurs during periods of drought). In most cases, you'll need only an average reading of the static water pressure, the water pressure available when no water is running inside or outside your house. Your goal is to determine the lowest static water pressure the irrigation system is likely to encounter. That way, as you plan the system, you will know that enough water pressure will reach each sprinkler so it can function correctly.

You may have reason to think the pressure that your irrigation system will receive when it is in operation, the working pressure, will be a good deal lower than the static pressure. For instance, you may run the sprinklers while your family is using several water sources in the house. If that is the case, see "A Simple Flow Test," on page 28.

One way of obtaining static water pressure is to contact the local water company or municipality. This is usually not the best method because the reading they give you is only a sector average. If your home is at a lower or higher elevation, the number may not be accurate. Checking the static water pressure yourself is best.

However, if you live in a new development, a reading of the water pressure in your home using a pressure gauge may actually be less useful than the water company's estimate, because water pressure will drop as additional households are added to the system. Instead, ask the water company for its estimate of the future static pressure in your sector.

To check the pressure yourself, attach a water pressure gauge to an outside faucet. An irrigation-products supplier may lend you one, or you can borrow or rent one from a

SOME QUESTIONS TO ASK

During the course of planning an irrigation system, you may need to ask local utility companies or municipal authorities several questions. You might want to start with these.
■ Where is my water meter located?
■ What is the static water pressure for my sector? Is it expected to drop in the future; if so, to what level?
■ What is the size of my water meter?
■ What is the diameter of my service line?
■ Do I need a permit to install a lawn- and garden-irrigation system?
■ What local codes affect the installation of an underground irrigation system? (Codes can specify the type of pipe and other materials, the type and location of backflow prevention, and the method of tying in to the water main. Also ask whether a licensed plumber is needed for certain installations.)
■ Are there any underground cables I should be aware of when digging? (Sometimes these are surprisingly close to the surface. Contact electric, gas, phone, and cable TV companies for this information.)
■ Do regulations govern private irrigation on municipal property, such as the planting strip between the sidewalk and the street?

Using a water gauge is generally the best way to check the static water pressure of your home.

A CLOSER LOOK AT YOUR PROPERTY
continued

hardware store. Turn off all water-using equipment (clothes washer, dishwasher, indoor and outdoor faucets, and so on), and ask family members not to turn on the water or flush the toilet. Tightly screw the gauge onto an outside faucet, turn on the faucet completely, and note the results in pounds per square inch or psi.

If possible, take the readings in summer when the municipal water level is low. Take note of the pressure levels at different times of the day, then use the lowest one in your calculations because you want the irrigation system to be efficient even when water

SERVICE-LINE DIMENSION CHART

Example: If your service line is galvanized steel pipe and it takes 4 inches of string to encircle it, the size of your line is 1 inch.

Length of String	2¾"	3¼"	3½"	4"	4⅜"	5"
Size of copper service line		¾"		1"		1¼"
Size of galvanized service line			¾"		1"	1¼"
Size of PVC (sched. 40) service line			¾"		1"	1¼"

pressure is not at its peak. Well owners should see "Wells and Pressure Tanks" page 28.

Write the lowest static water pressure reading on your planning sheet or installation guide. For proper system operation, water pressure should not exceed 80 psi. If yours exceeds this amount, install a pressure regulator.

2. CHECK WATER-METER SIZE: First locate the water meter. If you live in a cold climate, it is probably in the basement. In a warm climate, it may be near the street or just outside the house. If you don't know where it is, look it up on the property layout plan you received when you bought the house, or call the local water company or municipality.

Water meters usually come in three sizes: ⅝ inch, ¾ inch, or 1 inch. Your meter's measurement should be stamped on the meter. If not, contact the water company. Write down the water-meter size next to the static water pressure. If your municipality does not use water meters or if you use a well or pressure tank, you won't need to note this factor.

3. FIND SERVICE LINE DIMENSIONS: The service line is the main water pipeline running from the street to your home. You need its inner dimensions in order to determine water capacity. The water company or municipality might have this information, especially if your home is new. If not, it is easy to check the measurement yourself.

The service line measurement should be taken immediately before the water meter. If you don't have one measure the pipe running from the street into the house. To determine the circumference of the line, wrap a piece of string around the pipe, then measure the length of the string. The diameter of the

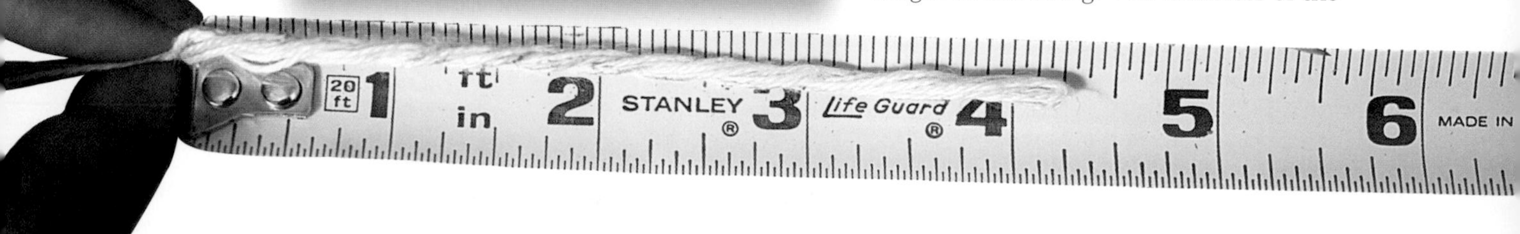

Water meter size is usually stamped on the surface (top). To find the inner dimension of the service line, wrap a piece of string around the pipe (center), then measure the string (bottom). Use the chart above to convert the measurement to the pipe size.

WATER CAPACITY IN GALLONS PER MINUTE (GPM)

Table 1: For Systems With a Water Meter (75-foot copper service line, or less)

Size of Water Meter	Size of Service Line	Static Water Pressure (psi)										
		30	35	40	45	50	55	60	65	70	76	80
5⁄8"	1⁄2"	2.0	3.5	5.0	6.0	6.5	7.0	7.5	8.0	9.0		
5⁄8"	3⁄4"	3.5	5.0	7.0	8.5	9.5	10.0	11.0	11.5	13.0		
3⁄4"	3⁄4"	6.0	7.5	9.0	10.0	12.0	13.0	14.0	15.0	16.0	17.5	18.5
3⁄4"	1"	7.5	10.0	11.5	13.5	15.0	16.0	17.5	18.5	20.0	21.0	22.0
3⁄4"	1 1⁄4"	10.0	12.0	13.0	15.0	17.0	18.0	19.0	21.0	23.0	24.5	26.0
1"	3⁄4"	6.0	7.5	9.0	10.0	12.0	13.0	14.0	15.0	16.0	17.5	18.5
1"	1"	10.0	12.0	13.5	17.0	19.5	22.0	23.5	25.0	26.0	28.0	29.0
1"	1 1⁄4"	12.0	15.5	17.5	21.0	23.5	26.0	28.5	30.5	32.5	34.0	35.0

Table 2: For Systems Without a Water Meter (75-foot copper service line, or less)

Size of Service Line	Static Water Pressure (psi)										
	30	35	40	45	50	55	60	65	70	76	80
1⁄2"	2.0	3.5	5.0	6.0	6.5	7.0	7.5	8.0	9.0		
3⁄4"	6.0	7.5	9.0	10.0	12.0	13.0	14.0	15.0	16.0	17.5	18.5
1"	10.0	12.0	13.5	17.0	19.5	22.0	23.5	25.0	26.0	28.0	29.0
1 1⁄4"	12.0	15.5	17.5	21.0	23.5	26.0	28.5	30.5	32.5	34.0	35.0

interior of the pipe is less than its outside circumference and depends on the thickness of the material from which the pipe is made. Copper pipe, for example, is thinner than galvanized steel or schedule 40 PVC pipe. It is easy to tell the pipes apart. Copper pipe is metallic and reddish bronze; galvanized pipe is a grayish metal; PVC pipe is plastic.

ELEVATION CONSIDERATIONS

The water-capacity calculations in Tables 1 and 2 above are based on the assumption that your yard is relatively flat. For each 1 foot rise in elevation, there is a corresponding loss of 0.433 psi of pressure. Likewise, for each 1 foot drop, there is a 0.433 psi gain in pressure. Any major differences in elevation in your yard will affect the working pressure. To take this into account, add or subtract the appropriate factor and recalculate the water capacity in gallons per minute for that sector only. For example, if your static water pressure measured at the house is 55 psi, and one sector of the backyard is 10 feet higher than the house, subtract 5 psi (10 feet x 0.433, rounded off), which gives you a water pressure of 50 psi. Now use the charts again to recalculate the water capacity for that sector.

To determine the inner size of the service line, use the Service-Line Dimension Chart on the opposite page. Jot down this measurement next to the static water pressure and the water-meter size.

4. CALCULATE WATER CAPACITY: If you are having your system professionally designed, take the measurements (static water pressure, water-meter size, and service-line size) to the irrigation specialist. If you are designing the system yourself, consult the water-capacity tables above. Use Table 1 if you have a water meter; Table 2 if you do not.

To use the tables, find your water-meter and service-line sizes in the left columns, then find the static water pressure along the top. The point where the two lines converge gives you the approximate water capacity. For example, if the water meter measures 1 inch, your service line is 3⁄4 inch in diameter, and the static water pressure is 55 psi, Table 1 shows you will have a maximum flow of 13.0 gpm for each circuit.

Note that the tables are based on a 75-foot copper service line. If your line is PVC, add 2 gpm. If the line is galvanized, subtract 5 gpm. If the service line is significantly longer than 75 feet, contact an irrigation supplier to determine a more specific calculation or see "A Simple Flow Test," page 28.

The water capacity you have determined indicates the maximum amount of water you can count on being able to use at any one

A CLOSER LOOK AT YOUR PROPERTY
continued

A SIMPLE FLOW TEST

If your service line (the length of pipe between the street and the house) is longer than 75 feet, or if it might be seriously corroded, the flow could be limited—which would result in considerable loss of pressure. The values given in the water-capacity tables (see page 27) assume a static water pressure that is the same as the working pressure of the system. But if the pressure that is actually available when the water is running is severely reduced, the reading you took will not accurately reflect the flow. A quick flow test roughly shows the actual number of gallons per minute of working or operating pressure. Place a bucket of a known size under an outside faucet, turn on the water full force, and count the number of seconds it takes to fill the bucket to the brim. To calculate the number of gallons per minute, simply divide the bucket size in gallons by the number of seconds it took to fill, then multiply this total by 60 seconds. The result is the number of gallons per minute available at the faucet. Here is the formula.

$$\frac{Bucket\ size\ (gal.)}{Seconds\ to\ fill} \times 60 = gpm$$

For example, if a 2-gallon bucket fills with water in 10 seconds, the available flow is 12 gallons per minute.

WELLS AND PRESSURE TANKS

If your water is supplied by a pump or pressure tank, you will need another means of determining water capacity. Check the owner's manual to find the working pressure (in psi) and flow rate (in gpm) of the pump. Alternatively, locate the name and number of the pump and contact your well or pump dealer.

time. You'll need this figure when determining how many sprinklers or emitters you can include in one circuit.

DRAWING A PLAN

Whether you draw up the irrigation plan yourself or have a professional do it, you'll need a plot plan of your property. This plan must be as accurate as you can make it; overestimating the needs of your property can be expensive and underestimating them will result in an irrigation system that does not cover the entire area. To draw your plan you will need both plain paper and graph paper, pencils and erasers, a 50- to 100-foot tape measure, a spike, a stake or screwdriver, a ruler, and a compass.

OUTLINE BUILDING AND PROPERTY LINES: Start by locating, if possible, an existing property layout plan. You probably received one with your deed. If not, you can obtain a copy from the local building department or tax assessor's office. Remember, this plan may or may not include the area between your property line and the street, but if you want to irrigate that area, you'll need to take it into account. If your yard was professionally landscaped, you should have a plan of this as well.

Do not draw directly on any existing plan, but transfer its details to grid paper. Do not

assume these plans are accurate, since structures or plantings may not have been placed exactly as planned and any changes made over the years are probably not shown. Nevertheless, these plans are an excellent basis from which to begin drawing a plot plan.

Make a photocopy of the layout plan that most closely represents the current status of the yard, then recheck the measurements. If no layout plan is available, draw a freehand sketch of the property on plain white paper and pencil in measurements as you go along.

Start measuring with the house, noting all its outside dimensions. Then measure in both directions from the corners of the house to the property lines. A helper can hold one end of the tape measure while you hold the other. If you're doing it on your own, drive a stake or screwdriver through the loop at the end of

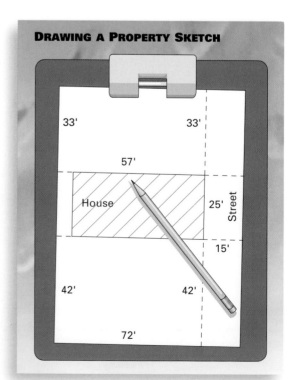

DRAWING A PROPERTY SKETCH

the measuring tape and into the ground to hold the tape in place.

Once you are sure of the measurements, transfer them to graph paper. An 11- by 17-inch sheet will provide plenty of space to work with, or tape two sheets of 8½- by 11-inch paper together. Most irrigation-system manufacturers provide a conveniently sized piece of graph paper in their installation guidebooks or with their parts list.

Using a convenient scale (1 small square to 1 foot, for example) and a pencil, trace the house onto the plan, then add the property lines. Don't be surprised if the property lines are not perfectly rectangular even if they appear to be so to the naked eye: few lots have perfect 90-degree angles at each corner. Don't hesitate to redraw the plan if you make any major errors. It is vital to have an accurate final version.

Once you have plotted the lot and house to your satisfaction, trace the property lines and house with a permanent marker so the details won't be accidentally erased as you work.

Now draw in the permanent features, such as patios, driveways, garages, toolsheds, walks, retaining walls, paving slabs, fences, flagpoles, pools, taking careful measurements of each.

SIGHTING BUILDING LINES

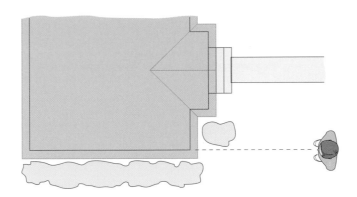

Use the corners of the house as reference points to make sure you've correctly located the features on the plan. Also indicate basement windows or other low windows. You won't want them constantly soaked by sprinklers.

You don't have to mark all measurements on the plan. They will be clearly indicated by the fact you've drawn to scale. If the plan is cluttered, erase less important measurements, leaving those you'll look at regularly when

INITIAL PLOTTING

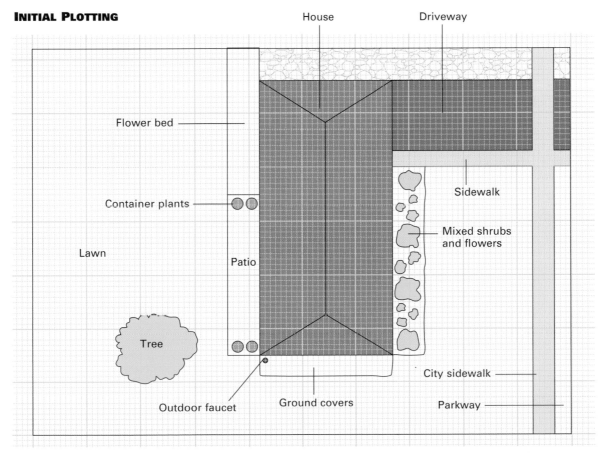

Scale: 1 square = 1'0"

A CLOSER LOOK AT YOUR PROPERTY
continued

planning, such as the length and width of driveways, walks, or flower beds.

INCLUDE PLANTS AND OTHER ELEMENTS: Your plot should also include all permanent plantings, including lawns, trees, shrubs, hedges, flower beds, ground covers, and vegetable beds. Be specific. If you know the names of trees and shrubs, write them down, using a legend if possible to reduce clutter. Take special note of any trees with low-hanging branches that could block spray patterns, and design your system to take their rain shadows into account.

Try to draw the landscape as it will be in the future. In the case of trees, for example, don't indicate only current height and spread but approximate size at maturity. As trees grow, they not only will need more water, but also are likely to block sprinklers from reaching parts of the yard. By planning for growth, you can put in sprinklers or emitters that will function for years to come. A good gardening reference book should provide the eventual height and diameter of trees and shrubs. If any elements of the landscape are planned but not yet installed, be sure to include them in the drawing.

Other elements you should incorporate are the water-supply line, water-meter location, and any outdoor faucets. If you use a pump and a well, show them. This information will help you decide where to connect the irrigation system to the supply line. Use a compass to determine which direction is north, and indicate this as well.

If you plan to use a sprinkler system, show the direction of prevailing winds, which may affect sprinkler placement. Finally, because you'll have to work around any underground cables, show them as well.

PLAN FOR SLOPE: If the yard is relatively flat, slope is not a concern. If it has a slope of more than 10 percent, however, there could be serious runoff problems if the proper equipment is not used and placed correctly.

In a carefully landscaped yard, most slopes have been eliminated or reduced through terracing and retaining walls. A moderate slope may have been solidified with ground covers. If any important slopes remain, they need to be measured.

To measure a slope you need a spirit level or a line level, a long string with a weight attached to one end, a tape measure, and a spike or screwdriver. You might also want an assistant because taking the measurements alone is awkward. Make a loop at one end of the string and attach it to the highest point of ground using a spike or screwdriver sunk into the soil. Have the assistant stand at the bottom of the slope and raise the string, holding it taut, until it is even with the higher ground. Be sure the string is fully horizontal by holding the level against the string or by checking the line level. Let the leftover string fall to the ground from your assistant's hand, using the weight to hold it taut so it forms a 90-degree angle.

Now measure both the length of string stretching from the high point of the lot to the assistant's hand and the distance from the assistant's hand to the ground. To find the slope, measured as a percentage, simply divide the rise (measure of height) by the run (measure of length) and multiply by 100.

For example, if the rise is 2 feet and the run is 12 feet, the slope would be 17 percent:

$$2 \div 12 \times 100 = 16.66\%$$

Sketch the slope onto the plan by shading it in with diagonal lines, and indicate the angle of the slope. If the slope is less than 10 percent, there is no need to show it.

DIVIDE YOUR YARD INTO CIRCUITS: Unless your lot is extremely small, you'll need more than one grouping of sprinklers or emitters (each grouping is called a circuit) for the front yard and more than one for the back. The number of circuits depends mostly on whether you will use a sprinkler system or micro-irrigation system (sprinkler

MEASURING SLOPE

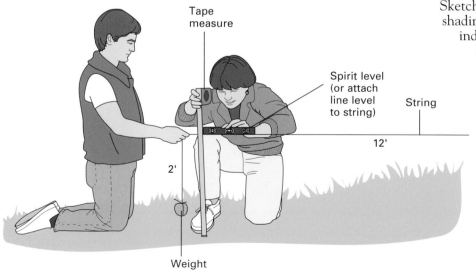

Tape measure

Spirit level (or attach line level to string)

String

12'

2'

Weight

systems use more water and, therefore, cover less territory). You will also need to consider the type of sprinkler or emitter you will use and the water requirements of different plants (for example, lawns versus flower beds).

Before deciding how many circuits you need, look at your landscape plan and sort plantings into coherent groups, keeping the following in mind.

■ Water plants in full sun separately from plants in shade because the former will dry out more quickly.

■ Lawns have different watering needs than most other plantings and often require different irrigation equipment. They should generally be watered separately.

■ Plants requiring infrequent, deep waterings, such as trees and shrubs, should be watered separately from plants that require frequent, shallow waterings, such as annuals and vegetables.

■ Trees and shrubs planted individually in a lawn can be watered using the lawn system, but take care to ensure they receive adequate moisture from all sides without blocking spray patterns.

DIVIDING THE PLAN ACCORDING TO WATERING NEEDS

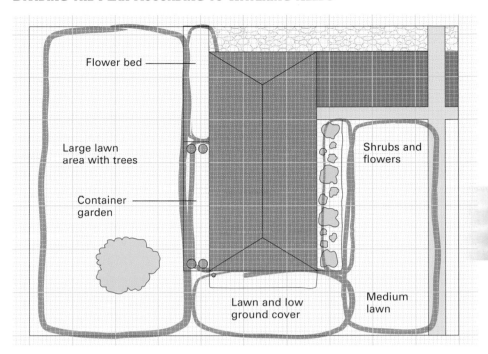

Flower bed

Large lawn area with trees

Container garden

Shrubs and flowers

Lawn and low ground cover

Medium lawn

■ In small yards, plantings with similar although not identical needs, such as ground covers, flower beds, and hedges, can be grouped together. In larger yards where several circuits are required anyway, they are best kept separate.

■ Container plants dry out more quickly than plants in the ground and should be watered separately.

■ Plantings with special needs should be kept separate. Roses, for example, should not have their leaves moistened. If you're using spray irrigation elsewhere, you may prefer to provide a separate micro-irrigation or bubbler circuit for the rose bed. Likewise, Xeriscaped sectors require less water than others and should be watered separately.

■ Problem areas, such as slopes, should be on individual circuits.

Taking these factors into account, divide the yard into areas with similar needs. Try to group the areas into squares or rectangles, which are easier to work with than odd-shaped zones. Label the areas according to the predominant vegetation: lawn, shrubs, ground cover. To divide these areas into their final circuits according to the type of irrigation and the kinds of sprayers you have chosen, look carefully at the next two chapters, "Sprinkler Irrigation" (page 33) and "Micro-Irrigation" (page 59).

ASSESSING GUARANTEES

The materials used in building irrigation systems are increasingly resistant to breakage and damage. Most companies now offer two- to five-year guarantees. Some even have limited lifetime warranties on certain parts.

Commercial-grade products generally cost about one-third more than residential-grade components, but are better quality, longer lasting, and less subject to breakage. The guarantee should indicate this.

Product guarantees cover the equipment, not the installation. If you install the system yourself, make sure there are no leaks or breaks. If you hire a contractor, get written guarantees on workmanship, good for at least two years.

Sprinkler irrigation can make watering child's play. Planning is the key. The sprinklers on this lawn were sized and placed properly so the spray patterns overlap to ensure an even distribution of water.

SPRINKLER IRRIGATION

For most people, lawn and garden irrigation means an inground sprinkler system, also called high-pressure irrigation. It is by far the most popular method of irrigating residential properties and will undoubtedly remain so. High-pressure irrigation requires effort to plan and install, but it is not necessarily much more work than a micro-irrigation system, because there are fewer parts. Once it is up and running, it offers many years of nearly maintenance-free service. The system can be automated so that it practically runs itself.

In this chapter you'll find specifics about planning and installing a sprinkler system. You'll learn about selecting components, sizing the system, choosing and installing valves, and putting the system in. Read carefully even if you plan to use professional services for certain aspects of your installation, such as planning or trenching. Understanding how sprinkler systems operate will help you make important decisions and avoid expensive mistakes.

SELECTING COMPONENTS

There are an abundance of high-pressure irrigation systems on the market, each offering a wide range of components. Some companies feature more than fifty different spray head nozzles alone. The basic information here will help direct your choice. First, you should understand how high-pressure irrigation works and how to use a system safely.

PLASTIC OR METAL?

It used to be that all sprinkler parts were made of metal, but that is less and less often the case. Irrigation pipes are now almost always made of plastic and so, increasingly, are sprinkler components. Don't assume that metal parts are necessarily longer lasting or more resistant to breakage or to the elements. Plastic nozzles and pop-up spray heads, for example, are at least as durable as brass ones and often even superior to them, yet are frequently less expensive. If in doubt about whether metal or plastic would be best in your case, consult an irrigation supplier.

CHOOSING THE WHOLE ENSEMBLE

A sampling of sprinkler heads. Top row (left to right): Pop-up impact head, pop-up spray head on lateral flex tubing, and gear-driven rotary head. Bottom row: Impact head, spray head on rigid plastic pipe, bubbler on rigid plastic pipe, and stationary spray head on flexible riser.

High-pressure irrigation systems take advantage of a home's high water pressure to water lawns and gardens. Water is carried underground through pipes to individual sprinklers or heads and released under high enough pressure to produce a spray. The coverage of each head varies according to the type of sprinkler, but each one requires a specific amount of pressure. That's why it is important to know the static water pressure for your home's system, and the gallons per minute used by each sprinkler head. You can run only so many sprinkler heads before the pressure drops so low the system no longer operates efficiently.

It is always worthwhile to get advice from an irrigation supplier. Even if your goal is to design and install the system yourself, a supplier with a thorough knowledge of the product line can help you avoid pitfalls.

Whenever possible, purchase products from the same manufacturer, particularly sprinkler heads and components. This is especially true within a given circuit. Not only does this ensure parts are compatible, but they will be easier to replace. Parts from the same manufacturer may also be color-coded, an aspect you'll find helpful when you're working with them. As you install the system, write down the name and model number of all the parts, and note where in the plan they go. If you need a replacement part, it is easier to pull out your plan than to try to find a tiny serial number stamped on a muddy underground sprinkler housing.

Because they require different pressures to operate effectively, try not to mix and match sprinkler types unless the manufacturer suggests it can be done. Bubblers should go on one circuit, rotary sprinklers on another, and spray heads on yet another. Full- and part-circle rotary heads can be mixed, as long as you purchase flow-balanced nozzles (see "Spray Heads," page 36). Lawn heads and shrub heads, both spray heads, can be combined. Low- and high-capacity sprinklers need to be on separate circuits.

Irrigation systems are constantly being updated. The examples here represent state-of-the-art materials at the time of publication, but don't assume they are still the best or most appropriate. Always check which components are available and the advantages of each before deciding what you need.

SAFETY CONSIDERATIONS

As you design your system, always keep safety in mind. You'll want to ensure that risers and pipes do not trip visitors. And you'll want to prevent any damage to your system from garden equipment.

■ Keep lawn sprinklers low. One reason why high-pressure irrigation is so popular and so safe is that most of its components are underground. There are no hoses or pipes running over the lawn and walks to cause people to trip. Sprinkler heads can remain level with the ground when not in operation. If they are above ground, they can be in spots where foot traffic is unlikely, such as among shrub plantings and flower beds or along fences and walls. It is especially important to set lawn sprinklers at the right level. In a sea of grass, they are often almost invisible, so any sprinkler even slightly above soil level could cause people to trip.

■ Keep sprinklers out of harm's way. Another consideration is lawn-mower damage. If a lawn-mower blade hits a sprinkler, not only can the impact break expensive parts, but flying pieces of plastic or metal could harm the mower operator or passersby. Check pop-up heads periodically to make sure they retract efficiently.

Place any aboveground parts, such as stationary shrub heads or bubblers, far from danger. If you have any doubts about the location of an above ground part, such as a riser within a bed but only inches from the lawn-mower's path, use a head with a flexible base (below right). When bumped, it will be pushed out of the way rather than snapped off or broken.

■ Set pipes deep enough so there is no danger of breakage during any digging. Set them 8 to 12 inches deep in flower beds and other areas where occasional digging is likely and even deeper (18 inches) under vegetable beds where digging is a certainty. Do not install pipes in beds where rototillers or other soil-turning equipment are used.

■ Cover all the valves. Valves and their numerous connections can present safety problems. Place underground valves in a specially designed inground valve box with the top set flush with the ground (below left), allowing easy access for repairs or adjustments, but creating no danger for passersby or impediment to mowing. The lid should be set firmly on the valve box at all times. Aboveground valve groupings, with

their various pipes arching in and out of the ground, are especially dangerous. Because they are not visually pleasing, place them in out-of-the-way spots, behind shrubbery, or in a seldom-used corner of the yard. For added safety and to hide valve groupings completely from sight, cover them with a wooden box or shock-resistant container, or place them under a porch or in a toolshed.

■ Flag danger spots. Any part of the irrigation system that cannot be placed out of range of foot traffic should be made highly visible with brightly colored reflective paint, a colorful ribbon, or a flag, rather than camouflaged. Be sure to flag danger spots during installation.

■ Look out for slippery zones. Excess water is harmful to plants and can create dangerously slippery conditions. Design your sprinkler systems to water lawns and gardens, not walks and driveways. Of course, some overlap is often inevitable, so run the system when foot traffic is unlikely, such as late evening or early morning. Use nonskid materials for walks that are subject to periodic irrigation spray, especially if the surface is sloped.

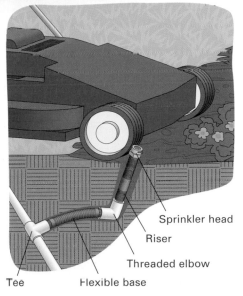

SWING JOINT ASSEMBLY

Sprinkler head

Riser

Threaded elbow

Tee

Flexible base

SELECTING COMPONENTS
continued

GETTING THE PIPE SIZES RIGHT

Landscape-quality pipes in both PVC and polyethylene, or poly, are available in various sizes; the most common are ¾ inch, 1 inch, and 1¼ inch. Valves also come with variously sized openings. Be sure to get pipes and valves large enough for your needs; if you don't, your sprinklers will not be able to do their job.

Contrary to what many people think, stepping down in pipe size decreases water pressure rather than increasing it. In some cases you may want to move from a smaller to a larger diameter pipe. For instance, to install 1¼-inch pipe even if your service line is only 1 inch.

Take the following factors into account when choosing pipe size: the total number of gallons used by the sprinkler heads, the total length of your pipes, the type of pipe, the number of elbows used, and elevation changes.

Your best bet is to take all your plans to a qualified irrigation dealer, who can tell you what size pipe to use.

CHOOSING SPRINKLER HEADS

There is a wide range of sprinkler heads on the market. Take a close look at each of the basic categories—spray, rotary, and bubbler heads—to decide how to plan your system.

SPRAY HEADS: These popular, versatile heads produce a broad band of spray in either a full or partial circle, depending on the spray radius you chose. The heads irrigate their entire coverage area at one time. although they are sometimes called mist heads because their spray can appear mistlike, they actually produce droplets much larger than mist. They cover a moderate radius, usually 8 to 15 feet, so you will need more spray heads than rotary heads to water a given surface. Their smaller range, however, makes them more adaptable than rotary heads.

If you need more than one spray pattern (see "Sizing the Sprinkler System," page 42) in a circuit, look for spray heads with balanced flow (also called flow adjustment or matched precipitation rate). This means the pressure in each is adjusted according to the area it covers. A flow-balanced half-circle head sprays only half as many gallons of water per minute as a full-circle head on the same circuit, and a quarter-circle head sprays only one-fourth as much. A quarter-circle head spraying as much water as a full-circle head will have inundated its small area whereas the full-circle head is just beginning to moisten its sector.

Spray heads can be stationary heads and pop-up heads. Both of these categories can further be divided according to their use: flush heads (set level with the soil) and shrub heads (set on risers).

■ STATIONARY SPRAY HEADS: These have no moving parts to break, making them almost trouble free. Flush stationary heads were once the industry standard for lawns and low ground covers, but are now rarely used.

Top: Pop-up spray heads are commonly used on medium to small areas. Right: Flush stationary spray heads should be used only in lawn areas with short grass.

CHOOSING THE BEST SPRINKLER FOR YOUR NEEDS

| | Spray Heads | | Rotary Heads | | |
	Lawn Head	Shrub Head	Impact or Gear	Multistream	Bubblers
Small lawns	Yes	No	No	No	No
Medium lawns	Yes	No	Yes	Yes	No
Large lawns	Sometimes	No	Yes	Sometimes	No
Flower beds	No	Yes	No	No	Yes
Ground covers	Low ones	Yes	Low ones	Low ones	Yes
Shrubs	No	Yes	No	No	Yes
Isolated areas	No	No	No	No	Yes
Slopes	Low gallonage	Low gallonage	Yes	Yes	No

Their major flaw is that the lawn has to be kept cut short so the spray will not be blocked by tall grasses. Also, in northern climates where most lawn grasses are of the creeping type, the immobility of the spray head leaves it vulnerable to clogging by invasive rhizomes.

Stationary shrub heads are set on risers in order to spray above shrubs, flower beds, ground covers, and other medium height vegetation. When the head is set higher than the tallest branch there is no foliage to block the distribution of water. The height is fully adjustable. The riser pipe is cut as needed, taking into account the mature heights of the plants. Shrub heads are usually placed in unobtrusive spots away from foot traffic because their elevated position makes them a safety hazard and susceptible to breakage. To reduce both problems, use a flexible joint at the base of the riser. Shrub heads can use the same type sprinkler as flush heads, but there are also specially designed shrub sprinkler heads that direct the spray at a lower angle so less water is lost to evaporation.

Top: This pop-up spray head is adjusted to deliver a direct spray over a quarter- to half-circle area. Bottom: Rotary heads are designed to send out strong streams of water over great distances.

Stationary shrub heads are used to water hedges, shrubs, and foundation plantings.

■ POP-UP SPRAY HEADS: Most lawn sprinkler systems use pop-up heads. Like stationary flush heads, pop-up heads are generally set flush with the soil, but they contain a stem with a nozzle that rises when the water is turned on, then sinks back into the body of the sprinkler when the system is off. The pop-up action allows the heads to reach above nearby plants yet remain unobtrusive when not in use. Pop-up heads are most popular for lawns and low-growing ground covers, but taller models can be used with small shrubs, vegetation of moderate height, and annuals. Pop-up heads can also be put on risers for use with tall shrubs.

Pop-up heads are available in various heights, ranging from 1 to 12 inches. If you're

SELECTING COMPONENTS
continued

An anti-backsplash device protects neighbors and passersby from stray spray.

looking for a specific height, especially among the taller models, make sure the manufacturer you choose carries them. For short-mown lawns, 2-inch or even 1-inch pop-up heads are perfectly acceptable, but for the typical 3-inch tall lawn, 3-inch or 4-inch heads are more appropriate.

Although water pressure pushes the pop-up nozzle out of its casing, gravity is not always sufficient to retract it. That's why pop-up sprayers of more than 2 inches in height are generally spring-loaded. Both gravity nozzles and spring-loaded nozzles contain few moving parts that are subject to breakage. Both are designed to keep out dirt because soil particles can clog the pop-up action. If the nozzles become clogged, however, you can easily take them apart for cleaning.

ROTARY HEADS: Also known as stream heads, rotary heads cover the largest area of any sprinkler. Rather than supplying a sheet of water and irrigating their entire sector at once, rotary heads send out a high-velocity stream of water in one or two directions, then rotate slowly to cover the entire area. Because only part of the surface is irrigated at any one time, the flow is concentrated, allowing the rotary head to throw water much farther than a spray head can. Most rotary heads cover a minimum radius of 16 to 22 feet and a maximum of 40 to 48 feet, considerably more than the range of 8 to 15 feet for a spray head.

Because it is difficult to design a nozzle that can simultaneously spray an area 45 feet from the head and the area within a few feet of its base, rotary heads usually have two nozzles: a long-range nozzle for the outer limits of its area and a short-range nozzle for the inner part. In part-circle heads, both nozzles point in the same direction, giving the impression of a solid stream that waters from the head to the outer limits of its coverage area. Some

SPRAY PATTERNS

Sprinkler heads of all types (spray, rotary, and bubbler) are available in different patterns, the best known of which is the full circle. But half-circle and quarter-circle patterns are just as useful because they allow you to place sprinklers on the periphery of the zone they will irrigate, out of the way of lawn mowers and foot traffic, rather than in the center. Three-quarter, two-third, and one-third patterns are also available, as are heads with adjustable spray patterns, often called VAN heads.

Special spray-pattern nozzles for specific uses include strip nozzles used to water long, narrow strips such as parkways or narrow raised beds. They come in four patterns: center, side, end, and square.

Center strip sprinklers spray in two directions at once. Side strip sprinklers also water in two directions but are placed along the edge of the strip. End strip sprinklers water in only one direction. The square strip sprinkler is designed for wider strips; it waters in all four directions from its center placement.

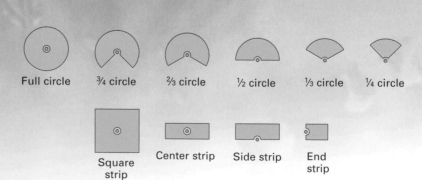

Full circle　¾ circle　⅔ circle　½ circle　⅓ circle　¼ circle

Square strip　Center strip　Side strip　End strip

short-range rotary heads have only one nozzle, because the area they cover efficiently falls within the range of one nozzle.

Rotary heads apply water more slowly than do high-gallonage spray heads, a boon for slow-to-drain clay soils. However, this means they need to run about four times longer than spray heads, which can cause problems in areas with water restrictions. Also, rotary heads lose more water to evaporation than spray heads do. On the positive side, you will need fewer rotary heads than spray heads to cover a given space.

Individually, rotary heads are less efficient than spray heads, but because you use fewer of them, a system with rotaries will usually waste less water than a system with spray heads. If your area is subject to strong winds, rotaries will waste more water because the water from them is more susceptible to getting blown off course and to evaporating.

Rotary heads are very popular in public parks but less so in residential areas. Few homes have the large expanses of unobstructed lawn or ground cover that rotary heads water so efficiently. Full-circle heads, which typically cover a minimum diameter of 40 feet, are especially ill-adapted for an average home landscape, but half- and quarter-circle rotary heads placed against walls or fences or in corners can be useful for large square or rectangular lawn areas.

Rotary heads can be either pop-up or stationary. Stationary rotary heads on risers of varying height are used on the periphery of large-to-medium lawns and planting areas. Pop-up rotary heads installed flush with the ground are usually set into lawns.

■ IMPACT SPRINKLERS: The best known and most frequently used rotary head is the impact drive, or impulse sprayer. It uses a spring-loaded drive arm which, when pulled into the stream of water by the spring, is deflected sideways, giving a jerky rotational movement and that familiar *sh-sh-sh* sound. Most impact sprinklers are almost fully adjustable and can cover a full circle or any part of one. For part-circle use, look for impact heads with a built-in antibacksplash device to keep them from watering sectors you want kept dry.

Metal impact heads generally require a minimum static water pressure of 40 psi to operate efficiently. If your system has a static water pressure of 40 psi or less, use impact plastic heads.

Multistream rotary heads produce fingerlike streams of water and rotate slowly to cover their entire zone.

SELECTING COMPONENTS
continued

■ GEAR-DRIVEN SPRINKLERS: Gear-driven pop-up rotary heads are becoming more popular. They include a series of gears that drive the rotary stream in a smooth and nearly noiseless pattern. The gears are hidden in an underground casing. Choose one with a closed-case design, which keeps out dirt. Most gear-driven drives are fully adjustable from full- to part-circle patterns and cover about the same surface as impact heads.

■ MULTISTREAM ROTORS: Producing several streams that rotate slowly to cover their entire trajectory, multistream rotors don't reach as far as other stream rotors. Multistream rotors cover more surface than spray heads and are best reserved for intermediate surfaces, from about 16 to 31 feet. There are both shrub sprinkler rotors and pop-up lawn sprinklers in this category. They are usually adaptable to full- and part-circle needs through interchangeable nozzles.

BUBBLERS: The bubbler, or flood head, is related to the spray head but is designed to deliver a large quantity of water to a relatively small area, usually a circumference of only about 5 feet. The name *bubbler* comes from the sound the water makes as it gushes out of the head. Bubblers should be raised high enough from the ground (usually about 4 to 6 inches) so they won't get clogged. Most are adjustable to emit anything from a full flow to a light trickle. Most are full-circle heads, but some offer part-circle functions. Bubblers are useful for small areas of medium-height vegetation. Because they water only the soil

Bubblers soak the soil around them, covering only a small surface. They are usually used for shrubs and ground covers.

LOW-GALLONAGE HEADS

Unless otherwise specified by the manufacturer, you can assume sprinklers are of standard gallonage and designed for normal water pressure.

Low-gallonage heads are intended for areas where water pressure is moderate to low (a static water pressure of less than 40 psi) or where water conservation is a priority. Because they apply water at a slower rate than other sprinklers, they are ideal where the soil is mostly clay and subject to runoff. Some companies call these sprinklers low-pressure heads, a term better reserved for micro-irrigation applications, which operate at even lower pressure.

and not the foliage, they are an ideal choice for plants such as roses, which won't tolerate water on their leaves. However, they make poor choices for sandy soils, because they operate by flooding the surrounding area. In sandy soil this means the excess water drains away without reaching nearby plants. Place bubblers on separate circuits and, because they deliver water rapidly to a small surface, run them only for short periods. Bubbler heads are increasingly being replaced by micro-sprinklers (see "Micro-Sprinkler Heads," page 63).

CHOOSING PIPING MATERIALS

Although your home may have galvanized steel or copper piping, and municipal regulations may require the use of copper piping right up to the backflow preventer, irrigation piping is almost always made of plastic. It does not corrode over time and is both low in cost and easy to install. The two products currently in use are rigid PVC piping and flexible polyethylene piping (poly pipe). Each has its advantages; many irrigation systems use both. If your area's plumbing codes allow metal or PVC pipe use PVC. Metal pipe is more expensive and more difficult to install.

PVC PIPE: PVC (polyvinyl chloride), is practically unbreakable,

and landscape-quality PVC pipe is usually rated at 160 psi or better, making it very resistant to bursting. It is relatively unaffected by temperature change and is unlikely to be damaged by expansion and contraction in all but the coldest climates when placed at an appropriate depth. PVC is usually less expensive than poly pipe but will need more joints because it lacks flexibility. Each joint must be welded individually using a solvent, making installation time-consuming. PVC pipe is available in various lengths, but 20 feet is standard. Schedule 40 PVC is usually recommended for outdoor irrigation. Do not use leftover PVC pipe from indoor use.

POLYETHYLENE PIPE: Polyethylene, or poly, pipe is rapidly taking the place of PVC as the pipe of choice for home-irrigation systems. It is flexible and, as a result, easier to install. You can bend it slightly to go around obstacles instead of having to cut the pipe and add extra joints. Connections are easily made without messy solvents. In many cases, you can even avoid trenching by using pipe-pulling equipment. Poly pipe is sold in coils of various lengths. Use only landscape-quality poly pipe with an appropriate pressure rating.

Poly pipe does have a major flaw. Its strength is limited and it can burst under high pressure, especially during pressure surges. These commonly occur in the main line when the flow of water in a pipe is abruptly reduced, such as when a valve is shut. You've probably heard surges pound and vibrate in your home, but pressure surges can also occur silently. Over time, pressure surges can weaken poly pipe and cause it to crack. Poly pipe marked "NSF" is of guaranteed quality, while "non-NSF" pipe may have inconsistent wall thicknesses.

PVC AND POLYETHYLENE TOGETHER: There is no clear-cut answer as to whether PVC or poly pipe is the better choice. Some people prefer to use PVC throughout their system, trusting in its superior strength and durability. Increasingly, manufacturers suggest a combination of the two.

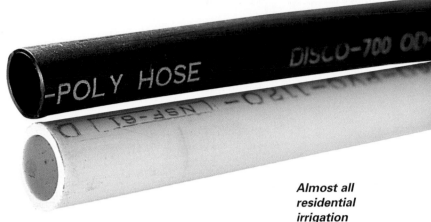

Almost all residential irrigation systems use polyethylene or PVC pipe.

Pressure surges are likely to occur only in the main pipes, not in the circuits themselves. You can use PVC for the supply lines leading to each circuit, and use poly pipe to link the sprinklers within each circuit.

In areas where freezing can occur to depths up to 12 inches, rigid PVC pipe can pulling apart as it contracts. Poly pipe, however, is compressed by the weight of soil in such deep installations. In these circumstances, some irrigation experts recommend using only metal pipe where a pressure surge is possible and, elsewhere, using loosely installed poly pipe inserted inside larger-diameter PVC pipe. The loose installation of the poly pipe means it can contract in cold weather, while the surrounding PVC pipe protects it from compression. Obviously, double piping is expensive.

Poly pipe connections usually call for easy-to-install clamps.

SIZING THE SPRINKLER SYSTEM

Now that you've sketched a simple plan and gathered the basic information about your home, yard, and water capacity, as well as the type of sprinklers and piping you intend to use, it is time to plot sprinkler locations on your plan.

PLOTTING AN IRRIGATION PLAN

Ideally, you should take the information you've gathered and the plot plan to an expert, who will draw a precise irrigation plan. If you intend to plot the plan yourself, have a specialist look it over and point out errors. Many will do so for free or for a modest fee. Making the plan entirely by yourself is risky. It is better to ask a specialist's advice now, even if you have to pay for it, than to spend hundreds of dollars later in renovations because of a faulty plan. In particular, it is important to get your pipe sizes right (see "Getting the Pipe Sizes Right," page 36).

To plot the plan yourself, you'll need a calculator, colored pencils, an eraser, a lead pencil, the manufacturer's equipment chart or list, a pencil compass, a ruler, and your plan.

It is important to have a copy of the manufacturer's equipment chart. You'll need it to determine the minimum and maximum spacing, the flow in gpm, and the spray pattern, for each sprinkler. These charts are usually divided according to the type of sprinkler (spray head, rotary, or bubbler) and include a list of valves, fittings, timers, and other parts.

Your plan should already show the buildings, plantings, walks, and other landscape elements. You should also have divided up the plantings into roughly square or rectangular areas according to type (lawns, shrub borders, ground covers); this is the basis for your plan of the different irrigation circuits.

To begin, draw in the sprinkler heads and calculate whether the water capacity in each sector is sufficient.

OVERLAPPING SPRAY PATTERNS

To irrigate adequately, spray patterns must overlap. Water loses force as it leaves the sprinkler head and may not reach the outer edge of the spray pattern sufficiently. If only one sprinkler covers an area, the center will receive more water than the outer areas. Also,

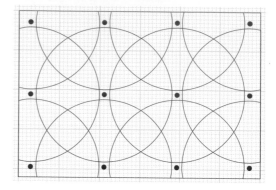

the outside perimeter of a spray pattern is apt to be disrupted by winds.

In general, place your sprinkler heads so water from one head will nearly reach the next head. You may want to space rotary sprayers a little farther apart to compensate for wind drift. The distance a sprinkler can propel water is called a "throw." For example, a spray head that has a diameter of 30 feet (and therefore a radius or throw of 15 feet) should be placed 15 feet (50 percent of 30 feet) to 18 feet (60 percent of 30 feet) from the head next to it.

You can adjust most spray heads to spray a radius of 10 to 15 feet; the average rotary sprayer can cover a radius of 25 to 45 feet; most bubblers reach 1 to 3 or 5 feet. If your static water pressure is lower than normal (40 psi or less), choose a lower radius as the appropriate spacing. The manufacturer's charts indicate the minimum and maximum spacing for each sprinkler.

PLOTTING SPRINKLER PLACEMENT

Plot sprinkler heads using a pencil compass adjusted to the appropriate spacing. If you're using 1 foot to one square on your graph paper and the sprinklers you're using have a throw of 10 feet, you could adjust the compass to a 10-square distance (10 feet). To cover the most surface with the fewest sprinklers, use the maximum recommended spacing at first (less if the site is windy or if the water pressure is lower than normal). If the area can not be divided evenly, place sprinklers closer together.

Begin plotting in the four corners of the squares and rectangles you drew on your plan, drawing a quarter circle in each. Position sprinklers evenly along the sides, drawing a half circle around each. If this doesn't cover the entire area, place sprinklers in the center and draw a full circle around each. Each circle should almost touch the head next to it. This

TRIANGULAR AND SQUARE SPACING

Irrigation plans are usually drawn using either square spacing or triangular (staggered) spacing. Square spacing, with heads located at each of the four corners, is the easiest to plot. There is, however, excessive overlap because some spots inevitably are watered by four sprinklers. Also, because sprinklers have to be placed relatively close (usually at 50 percent of the diameter or throw), more sprinkler heads are needed (the illustration below shows this). In triangular spacing, heads are located at each of the three points formed by a triangle. This means more surface is covered with less overlap, heads can be placed farther apart (usually at 60 percent of the diameter or throw, or even slightly more), and fewer heads are needed. For example, spray heads are typically placed at 15 feet or less in square spacing, 20 feet for triangular spacing.

To plot triangular spacing, first choose one side of a rectangular or square area as a baseline, then plot the two corner quarter-circle sprinklers, followed by equidistant half-circle sprinklers in between them as needed (so far, this is the same as square spacing). Next, draw lines upward from the center points between the sprinklers. Place the next row of sprinklers, not on the main line, as in square spacing, but at the half-space line. Continue to alternate the sprinkler heads between half-space and full-space lines. This will give you a triangular spacing. You may have some overshoot on the outside edges, but this water loss is compensated by the system's greater efficiency.

PLACING SPRINKLER HEADS

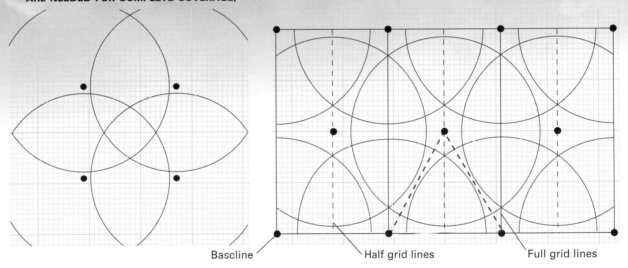

SQUARE SPACING (MORE HEADS ARE NEEDED FOR COMPLETE COVERAGE)

TRIANGULAR SPACING (COMPLETE COVERAGE SHOWN)

Baseline   Half grid lines   Full grid lines

will give you equidistant, or square, spacing. See "Triangular and Square Spacing," above for the more complex but more efficient triangular spacing.

STEP-BY-STEP PLANNING: Start with the largest of the squares or rectangles you drew on your plan, leaving the smaller and odd-shaped sections for last.

When you've completed the larger rectangles, position heads in small lawn areas, such as parking strips. These are usually watered by one or two rows of partial circles. Narrow spaces can be watered with strip nozzles (for lawns) or bubblers (for shrubs, beds, or ground covers).

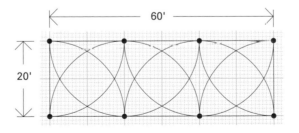

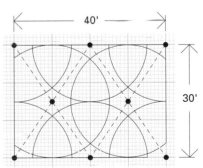

Two sample irrigation layouts: a 20- by 60-foot area covered by spray heads only (bottom left) and a 30- by 40-foot area covered by rotaries and spray heads (bottom right).

SIZING THE SPRINKLER SYSTEM
continued

PLOTTING THE IRRIGATION PLAN

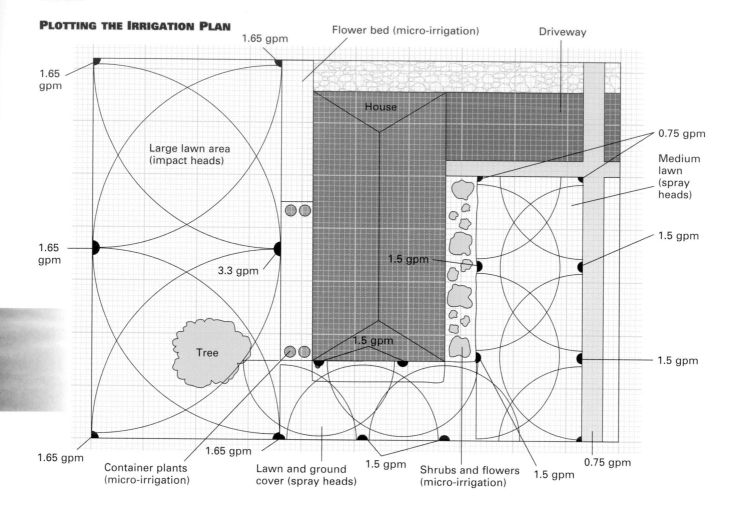

Flower bed (micro-irrigation)

Driveway

1.65 gpm

1.65 gpm

House

0.75 gpm

Large lawn area (impact heads)

Medium lawn (spray heads)

1.5 gpm

1.65 gpm

3.3 gpm

1.5 gpm

Tree

1.5 gpm

1.5 gpm

1.65 gpm

1.65 gpm

Container plants (micro-irrigation)

Lawn and ground cover (spray heads)

1.5 gpm

Shrubs and flowers (micro-irrigation)

1.5 gpm

0.75 gpm

Finally add sufficient shrub spray heads and bubblers to irrigate shrub areas, flower beds, and planters. Setting the sprinklers, where possible, at the back of the bed or along the periphery.

As you position sprinklers, jot down the details you'll need later to determine the circuits. As you draw circles and part circles indicating spray trajectory, show the placement of the head with a dot. Whole dots can indicate full-circle heads, and half or quarter dots can indicate half-circle and quarter-circle heads. Show the gpm rating for each sprinkler. You can find gpm ratings on the manufacturer's chart.

SPECIAL LAYOUT TECHNIQUES: Home landscapes rarely fit perfectly into equidistant sprinkler plans. You may have areas that need special planning. Here are ideas for coping with nonstandard elements.

■ ADJUSTABLE PATTERN HEADS: Rotary heads are generally fully adjustable, but most spray heads have fixed spray patterns: full circle, three-quarter circle, half circle, etc. If you have an awkward angle, consider using

adjustable pattern heads (VANs). Most adjust from 1 degree to 330 degrees.

■ FILL-IN HEADS: In many cases, equally spaced layout patterns cover most of a zone, but leave a few spots underwatered. Rather than struggling to design a perfect match, add a fill-in head. This sprinkler either is not located in the same symmetrical pattern as the others or has a smaller or greater coverage than the others. Sometimes such heads cause significant overlap, but this is better than leaving dry spots.

■ UNDESIRABLE OVERTHROW: Most homeowners have areas they want to keep dry, such as public sidewalks, yet some overthrow is inevitable, especially with triangular spacing. To keep a space spray-free use it as the baseline for your triangular layout. With a combination of quarter and half-circle heads, you can usually design the first line without overshoot. If you have two lines in the same sector where overthrow cannot be allowed (such as on a corner lot where two sidewalks intersect), you may need to modify the basic pattern with fill-in heads and part-circle nozzles.

■ OBSTACLES: One common problem is ensuring water reaches all parts of the garden in spite of obstacles. Even a flagpole can block enough spray to leave a dry zone on its far side. A triangular spacing of sprinkler heads with the obstacle at the approximate center of throw solves the problem nicely. When trees and other obstacles do not fall at the desired point of junction in an otherwise equidistant spray area, try adjusting the plotting; however, you will probably need fill-in heads with smaller ranges.

Similarly, groups of obstacles, such as clusters of shrubs, can be watered by outside heads positioned around them in a triangular pattern. Make sure that all spots are reached by at least part of the trajectory.

Remember trees and shrubs in lawns need more water than grass. You might want to put them on a separate circuit, provide them with micro-irrigation, or resort to occasional hand watering.

■ ROUNDED CORNERS AND CURVES: It is difficult to avoid overthrow at rounded corners, such as the curved entrance to a driveway, but you can reduce it with careful placement of sprinkler heads or use of adjustable heads. Curves are also difficult, but overlap is preferable to dry spots. The illustrations at right show various ways of using half-circle sprinklers to irrigate inside and outside curves.

■ HEDGES AND BORDERS: Shrubs, flower beds, and hedges are best watered on their own circuits with bubblers, shrub heads, or micro-irrigation, but can also be irrigated with flush heads placed on their periphery that can also water the lawn. If the hedge or planting is dense enough, water will not pass through it to soak the wall behind or the property next door.

DIVIDING INTO CIRCUITS

Once your landscape plan has spray trajectories well indicated, and all surfaces will receive adequate coverage, it is time to divide the plan into proper circuits or zones.

Except in small lots, the operating pressure for your property will not allow you to run all sprinklers at once, and even if it did, you probably wouldn't want to. After all, you

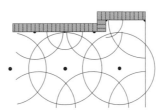
Working around a building

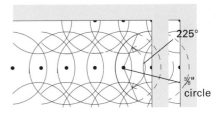
Avoiding watering a public sidewalk

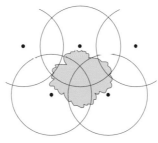
Using triangular spacing to work around an obstacle

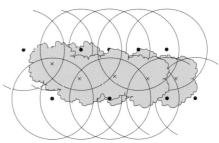
Using triangular spacing for an irregular group planting

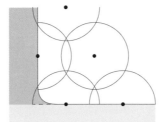
Reducing water loss at a rounded corner

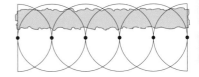
Watering hedges and lawns with a sprinkler on a riser

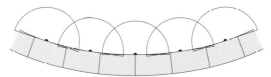
Irrigating around inside and outside corners

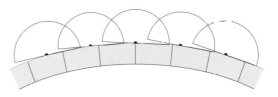

won't want a shady lawn that stays relatively moist to be watered as often as a planter box in full sun. This is why the plan has to be divided into individual circuits, each with a total operating pressure no greater than the system can support. Each circuit contains a varying number of sprinkler heads that operate together off a common valve.

Earlier, when you grouped the areas of the yard according to plant type and type of sprinkler required, then sketched in the

SIZING THE SPRINKLER SYSTEM
continued

DIVIDING A PLAN INTO CIRCUITS

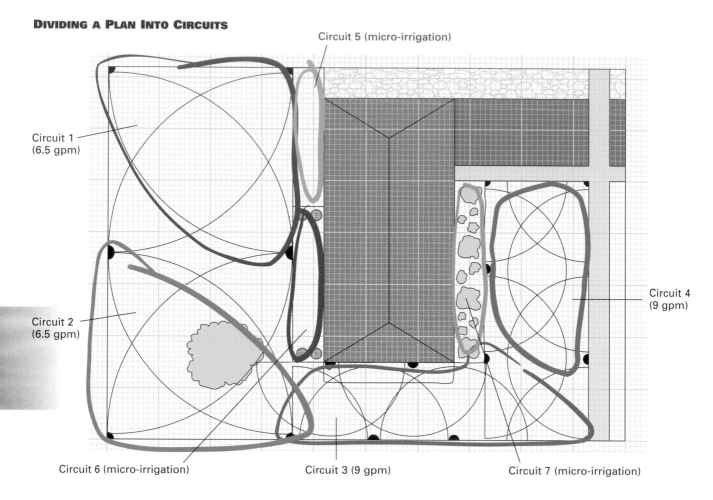

Circuit 5 (micro-irrigation)

Circuit 1 (6.5 gpm)

Circuit 2 (6.5 gpm)

Circuit 4 (9 gpm)

Circuit 6 (micro-irrigation)

Circuit 3 (9 gpm)

Circuit 7 (micro-irrigation)

sprinkler heads, you laid the groundwork for circuiting. Just remember that each circuit must contain only heads of the same type (rotary, spray, or bubbler). After that, simply verify that the circuits don't contain more sprinkler heads than the available pressure will allow.

DON'T FORGET

If you have to subdivide a proposed circuit, consider the following factors.
■ Plants with similar needs should be irrigated together.
■ Certain parts of the lawn may be shadier and need less irrigation.
■ If your yard is hilly, sprinklers that are at about the same elevation should be grouped together; otherwise the water in the system will drain out through the lowest sprinkler each time the sprinkler is turned off, possibly causing flooding.

To check this, add the gpm of all the sprinklers on each potential circuit, then add 10 percent (pressure loss due to pipe length and other factors) and compare this total with the capacity of your system (maximum gpm flow per circuit) that you found by using the tables on page 27. For example, if the total gpm of the sprinkler heads on a proposed circuit is 9, add .9 gpm (10 percent), for a total of 9.9 gpm. If your maximum gpm is 12, you can use the circuit as is. If the sum is 15 gpm plus 1.5, giving you a total of 16.5 gpm, divide the circuit into two. In borderline cases, be safe and divide the circuit.

As you determine the circuits, take into account any future plans. If you intend to add a flower bed or a few containers, leave some extra capacity in nearby circuits.

DETERMINING VALVE AND LINE LOCATIONS

Once circuits are established on paper, it is time to determine a path for bringing in water to supply the sprinkler heads. Start by plotting the water meter and the main service

PLOTTING VALVES AND LINES

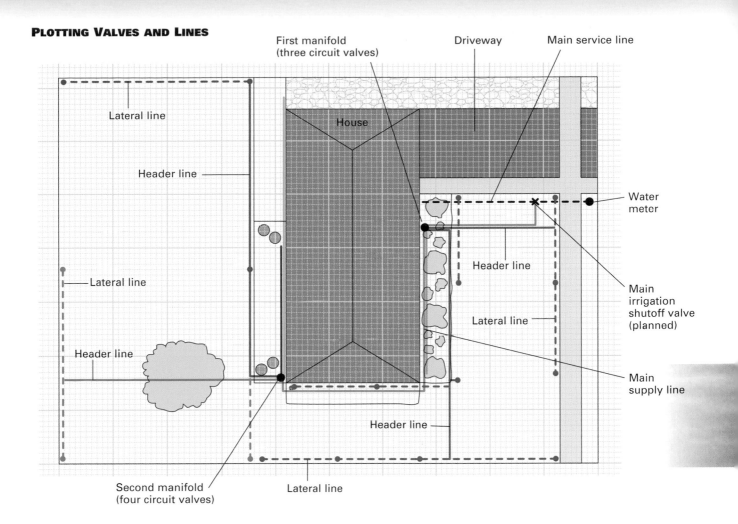

First manifold (three circuit valves) — Driveway — Main service line

Lateral line

Header line

House

Lateral line

Header line

Water meter

Header line

Lateral line

Main irrigation shutoff valve (planned)

Main supply line

Second manifold (four circuit valves) — Lateral line

Header line

line on the plan. You've already located the water meter (see "Check Water-Meter Size," page 26). The main service line usually follows a straight line from the water meter to the street if the water meter is indoors, or between the water meter and the point where the water line enters the house, if the meter is located near the street. Show the main service line on the plan as a dotted line.

MAIN IRRIGATION SHUTOFF VALVE LOCATION: Now determine where you'll be installing the main irrigation shutoff valve. This manual valve, used to turn the entire irrigation system on and off, should be installed on the house side of the water meter. It will be either in the basement or outdoors at some point between the meter and the house. In nonfreezing climates and under certain circumstances, you may also be able to install the main irrigation shutoff valve from an outside faucet (see "Hooking Up Near an Outside Faucet," page 52). Mark the planned main irrigation shutoff valve location on your irrigation plan.

CIRCUIT CONTROL-VALVE LOCATIONS: Each circuit will be operated by a separate control valve. Group these together in an accessible spot outdoors such as near a door or

patio, but away from heavy foot traffic. Each group of valves is called a manifold or valve grouping. In most cases, it is practical to have two manifolds, one for the front yard and one for the back and side yard.

To simplify installation, plan to put one manifold near the main service line. If you use outdoor faucet lines as a hookup, locate the manifolds near them. Mark the manifolds on your plan.

PLOTTING THE MAIN SUPPLY LINE: Next, determine the path of the main supply line that will link the two manifolds to the main irrigation shutoff valve, and mark this line on your plan. If your main irrigation shutoff valve will be located indoors, run the line outdoors first, then in opposite directions, one line leading toward the first manifold and the other around the house to the second manifold. If the shutoff is near the street, run the main supply line first toward the house, then toward the manifolds.

PLOTTING THE IRRIGATION PIPES: Because each circuit has a separate control valve, plot an irrigation pipe system for each. Start by drawing one header line per circuit. This main line will carry water to the lateral lines, so be sure not to connect sprinkler

SIZING THE SPRINKLER SYSTEM
continued

heads to it. To each header line, add lateral lines as needed to connect the sprinkler heads on that circuit. The following tips will help you plan.

■ Avoid forcing water to travel through too many turns, because pressure will be lost.

■ Avoid directing lines under established driveways and sidewalks.

■ Use a different colored pencil for each circuit.

■ Place header lines side by side so they can share a trench whenever possible to reduce digging.

■ Place lines 1 or 2 feet outside established flower beds and shrub plantings to avoid damaging roots when digging the trenches.

BACKFLOW PREVENTERS

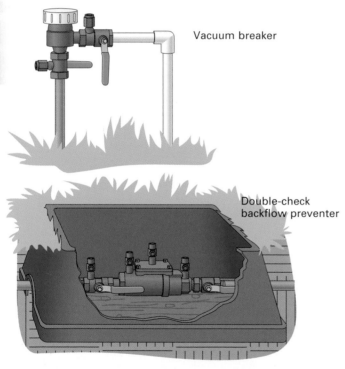

Vacuum breaker

Double-check
backflow preventer

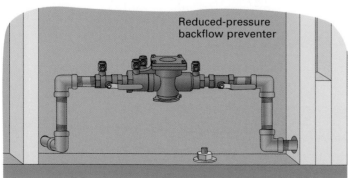

Reduced-pressure
backflow preventer

■ Plot lines about 3 feet from the house and other structures to avoid damaging pipes.

PREVENTING BACKFLOW: Sprinkler systems must include backflow prevention. When irrigation is suddenly turned off, siphonlike conditions can occur, sucking dirt, bacteria, funguses, pesticides, and other contaminants from around the sprinkler heads into the irrigation piping and, eventually, into your home's plumbing system. If sprinkler heads are located at a higher elevation than the manifolds, the danger is increased. Most municipal codes or water districts have specific requirements about backflow preventers, so check before you purchase.

ANTISIPHON VALVES: Many local codes require antisiphon valves on all subsurface irrigation systems. These are basically control valves that include a backflow prevention (antisiphon) device. They are available in automatic and manual forms. Most codes require you to install an antisiphon valve 6 inches above the highest lawn sprinkler. See "Installing Antisiphon Valves in a Manifold," page 54.

DEDICATED BACKFLOW PREVENTERS: Some municipalities require the control valves and the backflow prevention devices be kept separate. There are three commonly used types of backflow preventers.

■ VACUUM BREAKERS: These are the most common backflow preventers, usually installed 12 inches above the highest lawn sprinkler head. This height difference is vital, because the devices are effective only when they are higher than the sprinkler heads. They can't be used in hilly yards where sprinkler heads are at higher elevations than the control valves. Atmospheric vacuum breakers are inexpensive, but you'll need one for each circuit. Pressure-type vacuum breakers cost more, but you can use one for the whole system.

■ DOUBLE-CHECK BACKFLOW PREVENTERS: These can be installed above- or below-ground and are not affected by the height of the surrounding sprinklers. They are more expensive than vacuum breakers and are usually reserved for hilly terrain.

■ REDUCED-PRESSURE BACKFLOW PREVENTERS: These are mandatory in some areas. One will cover the whole system, although other backflow preventers may be required as well. They must be vented and cannot be installed below the ground.

PUTTING IT ALL TOGETHER

Now that your plan is drawn up, it's time to get organized. Prepare a parts list, stake out the yard, and gather your tools and materials.

PREPARING A PARTS LIST

If an irrigation professional planned the system, this step is done: A list of parts will be included with the plot plan. If you've done the work on your own, you can still take the plan to a specialist who can calculate your needs. If no local help is available, go over your plan carefully, measuring the length of both poly pipe and PVC pipe, and calculating the number of heads, couplings, tees, clamps, and amount of solvent. You'll also need a slip-type compression tee, control valves, and other components described on pages 50–57.

Most irrigation suppliers offer parts lists with blank spaces that you can fill in to indicate the number of each of the items you need. Use a pencil—you'll inevitably make changes.

STAKING OUT YOUR YARD

Before gathering materials, transfer your plan from paper to your yard. Use wood stakes or flags (an irrigation supplier should offer the latter in a variety of colors). If possible, color-code markers according to the colors on your plan and mark the name of the part on each marker to avoid confusion.

First stake out the main supply line, water meter, manifold locations, and valve positions. Then place markers for the header lines and lateral lines and, finally, each of the sprinkler heads.

Check the spacing of sprinkler heads by cutting a length of string to represent the proposed radius or throw, nailing or tying it to the stake or flag representing the sprinkler head, then walking the circle holding the string to see where water will reach. Its spray should touch or nearly touch neighboring heads. Make any necessary adjustments.

Now run string from the stakes to indicate the paths of the pipes. Doing so might well show places where you can use common trenches to save some digging or reveal overlooked obstacles. Finally, if you'll be using automatic controls (see page 79), stake out a

Colored flags, available at nurseries and irrigation supply outlets, help you to differentiate circuits when staking out your sprinkler system.

INSTALLATION TOOLS AND SUPPLIES

50-foot tape measure

Power drill

Mattock

PVC saw

Masonry bit

12-foot tape measure

Utility knife

Phillips/standard screwdriver

Pliers

Crimper

Flags

Plastic-pipe cutters

Layout string

PUTTING IT ALL TOGETHER
continued

PIPE FITTINGS

Pipe fittings for irrigation systems include a bewildering array of small parts. These are among the common ones.

POLY PIPE

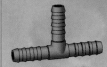

•Insert Coupling:
Connects two lengths of poly pipe.

•Insert Tee:
Connects three lengths of poly pipe.

•Combination Tee:
Attaches threaded riser between poly pipe and sprinkler.

•Insert Elbow:
Forms 90° angle using two pieces of poly pipe.

•Combination Elbow:
Forms 90° angle using poly pipe and PVC pipe.

•Insert Adapter:
Adapts threaded outlet to insert fitting for poly pipe.

•Stainless Steel Clamp:
Clamps insert fittings.

PVC PIPE

•Threaded Coupling:
Connects sprinklers to ½" riser.

•Slip or Socket Coupling:
Connects two lengths of same size PVC pipe.

•Reducer Bushing:
Connects two lengths of different size pipe.

•Slip or Socket Tee:
Connects same size PVC pipe at 90° from main line.

•Reducer Tee:
Attaches threaded riser between PVC pipe and sprinkler.

•90° Slip or Socket Elbow:
Forms 90° angle with same size PVC pipe.

•45° Slip or Socket Elbow:
Forms 45° angle with same size PVC pipe.

•Reducer Elbow:
Forms 90° angle and provides threads for threaded riser.

•Male Adapter:
Adapts threaded outlet to socket joint for PVC pipe.

BOTH POLY AND PVC PIPE

•Manifold Tee:
Connects control valves together into manifold.

•Threaded Riser:
Rises from pipe to sprinkler.

•Cutoff Riser:
Rises from pipe to sprinkler. Can be cut to desired height.

•Adjustable Riser:
Rises from pipe to sprinkler. Height can be adjusted.

•Flexible Riser:
Rises from pipe to sprinkler in high-traffic areas. Flexible.

•Drain Cap:
Cap for draining system.

•Drain Valve:
Automatically drains system when pressure is off.

•Slip-Type Compression Tee:
Connects irrigation system to main service line.

•Inground Valve Box:
Protects underground valves.

WORKING WITH PVC PIPE

First, cut the pipe with plastic-pipe cutters, a hacksaw, or a power miter box, and file off all burrs. Clean the area to be cemented, both fittings and pipe, with a dry rag, and apply a primer. Wait a few minutes for the primer to dry, then brush solvent cement around the outside end of the pipe and the inside of the fitting. Insert the pipe into the fitting, then give it a quarter turn to distribute the solvent. Hold for about 30 seconds, then wipe any excess solvent from around the joint. Allow it to set for the amount of time recommended on the cement can before applying water pressure; if the pipe is to be buried, wait at least 12 to 24 hours. If you

make a mistake working with PVC, cut off the pipe and fitting and redo the installation; PVC cement bonds pipe and fittings so solidly that they cannot be taken apart. To connect

PVC pipe to threaded piping, such as to a hose bib, simply cement it into an appropriately sized threaded adapter.

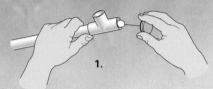
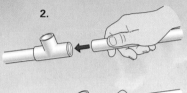

1. Apply primer to both fitting and pipe end, and allow to dry. Brush solvent cement on inside of fitting and outside of pipe.
2. Insert pipe and twist to tighten.
3. Wipe off any excess solvent.

---

trench leading from the main control valves to the system timer box, usually located in a garage, basement, or other protected area.

GATHERING MATERIALS AND TOOLS

You will need these tools and other items for installation: electrical tape, file, gravel, plastic-pipe cutter, hammer, hoe, utility knife, 1-inch pipe clamps for poly pipe, pipe plugs, pipe wrench, pliers, PVC solvent cement with primer and small paintbrush, dry rags, sand, screwdriver, shovel, string, tape measure, pipe

joint tape, tubing cutter (for metal pipe), and wooden stakes or flags. If the water hookup is in the basement, you'll need caulking compound or hydraulic cement, a power drill, and a 1-inch masonry bit.

INSTALLING THE SYSTEM

Give yourself plenty of time. It's better to work slowly and carefully than to rush and make mistakes.

Each step of the installation should be done with the water turned off. turn it off at the meter in the beginning stages and later at

---

WORKING WITH POLY PIPE

Poly pipe is easier to install than PVC. Cut it evenly to an appropriate length with a hacksaw, a knife, or pruning shears. Slip a stainless-steel hose clamp over the pipe and insert the fitting (tee, elbow, or coupling). If this is difficult to

do, soak the end of the poly pipe in warm water. This causes the pipe to expand slightly and become more supple, making installation easier. Now position the clamp over the ridged section of the fitting and tighten carefully.

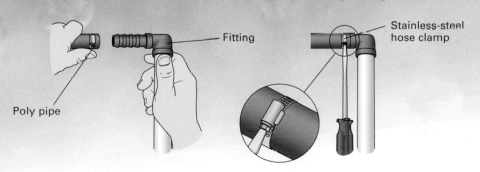

Poly pipe

Fitting

Stainless-steel hose clamp

PUTTING IT ALL TOGETHER
continued

the main irrigation shutoff valve. After each step, turn on the water to check for leaks and to flush the system.

Finally, at each threaded connection, apply pipe joint tape or paste. This not only will make the pipes fit together more easily, but will help create a better seal.

WATER HOOKUP: How you hook the irrigation system to the local water main depends on where your water meter is located. If you don't have a water meter, tie into the system after the shutoff valve for the main service line. To ensure proper pipe sizing, see "Getting the Pipe Sizes Right," page 36.

The instructions below assume you are using schedule 40 PVC pipe is used for this part of the system and that you are doing the work yourself. Some municipalities may require copper or metal piping and may also insist that a licensed plumber handle this part of the installation. Three of the most common main-line connections are described

here. Since codes vary, check them before installing any system.

■ HOOKING UP NEAR A BASEMENT METER: Turn off the water at the valve on the street side of the water meter. Using a tubing cutter (or a hacksaw for galvanized pipe), cut into the main service line just after the meter and before any existing pressure regulators, and remove about 3 inches of service line pipe. Insert a compression tee of an appropriate diameter (¾ inch, 1 inch, or 1¼ inch, depending on the size of the pipe). As you tighten the compression nuts, the tee will seal against leaking; no pipe threading or soldering is needed. Using a short section of PVC pipe, install a ball valve to act as the main irrigation shutoff valve.

Now install another length of pipe directly after the shutoff valve and add a manual drain valve. The shutoff can be closed during cold weather and the drain valve cap removed, draining this part of the system. Drill a hole through the foundation near where the backflow preventer and first manifold will be located, using a 1-inch masonry bit or a

TYPES OF WATER HOOKUPS

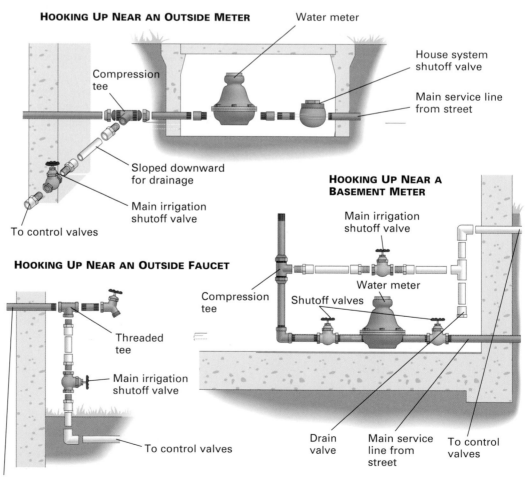

TRENCHING

Even if you use a pipe puller or trencher, you will have to do some digging by hand around buildings, corners, obstacles, and in flower beds. You'll have to dig trenches for the inground valve boxes and individual sprinkler heads, as well.

To pull PVC pipe, first glue all the pieces together and allow to dry completely (wait at least an hour).

For two days before digging, water hard soil moderately to soften it. To dig without a pipe puller or trencher, use a straight-edged shovel and dig V-shaped trenches 6 to 12 inches deep. A depth of 12 inches is best for main lines in cold climates, but 6 inches is sufficient as long as you install drain valves. In lawn areas, first remove the sod and put it to one side, then dig the trench and place the soil you remove on the other side.

Don't dig more trench than you can install pipe in during one session. Trenches dug up one weekend, with pipe installation planned for the next, could become a muddy mess or even collapse if you get rain in the meantime.

Pipe pullers should be run by experienced workers who will simply follow the lines you have indicated on the lawn. Make sure you are present to answer questions.

You can also rent an automatic trencher and operate it on your own. Get detailed instructions where you rent it. Use the trencher only through lawns, not flower beds or ground cover. It should not be operated near buildings, on steep slopes, or over any buried utility lines (check with your local gas, electric, telephone, and cable TV companies).

If possible, plan the system so you won't have to run lines underneath sidewalks, walls, or driveways. Otherwise, to work your way under such obstacles with the least effort, try digging underneath with a crowbar or forcing a length of 1-inch metal pipe through with a hammer. For a wide obstacle, such as a sidewalk, use waterpower.

DIGGING A TRENCH

Attach a hose to a length of pipe with a hose adapter. The pipe must be at least 12 inches longer than the width of the slab. Dig a trench on both sides of the spot where the tunnel should be dug, making sure there is enough room to maneuver the length of pipe. Put on safety goggles and gloves and turn on the water, pushing the pipe under the sidewalk and working it back and forth as the water pressure blasts a hole. After the irrigation pipe is inserted, solidify by pushing as much soil as possible under the slab.

USING WATERPOWER TO DIG A TUNNEL

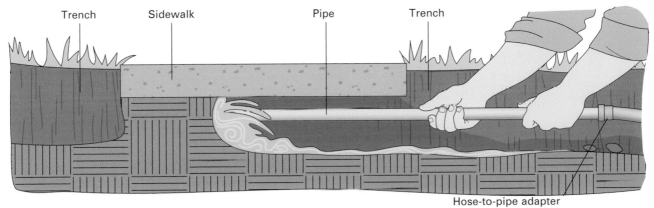

Trench   Sidewalk   Pipe   Trench

Hose-to-pipe adapter

PUTTING IT ALL TOGETHER

continued

INSTALLING ANTISIPHON VALVES IN A MANIFOLD

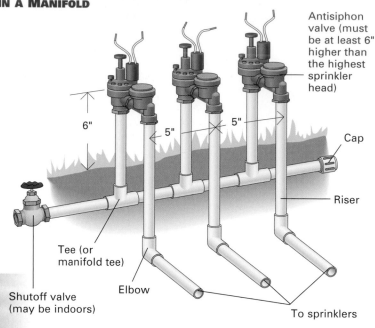

Antisiphon valve (must be at least 6" higher than the highest sprinkler head)

6"

5"   5"

Cap

Riser

Tee (or manifold tee)

Elbow

Shutoff valve (may be indoors)

To sprinklers

PRESSURE-TYPE VACUUM BREAKER

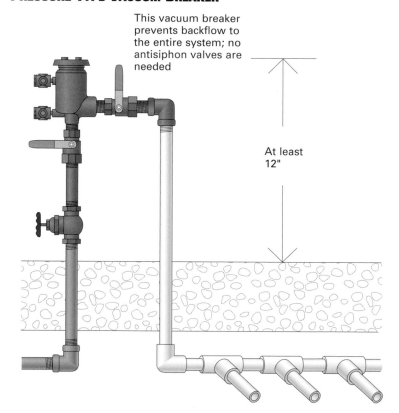

This vacuum breaker prevents backflow to the entire system; no antisiphon valves are needed

At least 12"

chisel. Don't make the hole any larger than necessary. Run the connecting pipe through the hole, sloping it slightly downward. Seal the wall with caulking compound or hydraulic cement. Turn on the water at the meter and open the main irrigation shutoff valve to flush the system and check for leaks.

■ HOOKING UP NEAR AN OUTSIDE METER: Turn off the water supply at the meter. Cut into the service line between the meter and the house wherever it is most convenient, near the street or near where the service line enters the house, depending on where you plan to install the first manifold. Insert and tighten a compression tee as described above. Install the main irrigation shutoff valve as above. For easier access, place the valve in an inground valve box. Now connect the main supply line and run it to the first manifold. Turn on the water at the meter and open the main irrigation shutoff valve to flush the system and check for leaks.

■ HOOKING UP NEAR AN OUTSIDE FAUCET: Use this method only in nonfreezing climates and then only when the line from the meter to the outside faucet is at least ¾ inch in diameter. Also, the length of pipe from the water main to the manifold should be no longer than 125 feet.

Shut off the water at the meter and remove the hose bibb. Install a threaded tee and reattach the bibb. Install the main irrigation shutoff valve. Connect the main supply line and run it to the first manifold. Turn on the water at the meter and open the main irrigation shutoff valve to flush the system and check for leaks.

INSTALLING VALVES AND RELATED COMPONENTS: The next step is to connect the necessary valves and install the wiring. If the water capacity of the system (see "Water Capacity in Gallons per Minute," page 27) is greater than 80 gpm, first install a pressure regulator to control the water pressure. Install it behind the main irrigation shutoff valve, between two lengths of pipe.

■ MAIN SUPPLY LINE: Cut a length of pipe to run from the shutoff valve to the first manifold, then another to run from the shutoff valve to the second manifold, linking the two with a tee. The main line should be installed in trenches at the same depth as the rest of the system. Try to grade it slightly so one section is lower than the rest and install an automatic drain valve (see "Automatic Drain Valves," above) at that point.

■ BACKFLOW DEVICE HOOKUP: Most irrigation systems use antisiphon valves and do not require a separate backflow device. If yours does require one, install it either between the main irrigation shutoff valve and the control valves (manifold) if it is intended

AUTOMATIC DRAIN VALVES

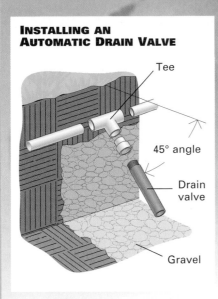

INSTALLING AN AUTOMATIC DRAIN VALVE

- Tee
- 45° angle
- Drain valve
- Gravel

Where temperatures drop below freezing, you must install automatic drain valves at the lowest point in each circuit. Drain valves are small threaded devices designed to remain shut when the water is under pressure and open when the water is turned off. They are easily attached to any underground line via a combination tee inserted in the pipe. They should be turned downward at a 45-degree angle from the line to allow for proper drainage. If you prefer, a short length of pipe can be slipped over the drain valve to keep it from blocking. Add at least one automatic drain valve per line, inserting it at the lowest point, so that no water remains standing in the pipes between waterings. This is essential in cold climates to prevent the pipes from cracking, and is valuable elsewhere as well.

In some cases, you might prefer to use a self-draining header rather than a drain valve. Many models of pop-up impact sprinklers, for example, have two inlets, one on the side one for water connection and on on the bottom for an automatic drain valve, allowing it to drain after each use. The bottom inlet can be plugged in warm climates, but a drain valve should be installed in each one in freezing climates. Place all automatic drain valves and self-draining headers over a small bed of gravel into which excess water can drain.

to control the entire system, or after the control valve if one backflow device is needed per circuit. Double-check backflow preventers are usually installed underground in an inground valve box. Vacuum breakers are necessarily placed above ground on risers at an appropriate height (usually 12 inches higher than the highest sprinkler head on the circuit). All backflow devices should be placed over a bed of 6 to 8 inches of gravel. Exact instructions for each are included with the product.

■ CONTROL VALVE HOOKUP: Control valves turn each circuit on and off automatically. They are generally grouped in manifolds, usually one in the front yard, one in the back.

■ INSTALLING ANTISIPHON VALVES: This installation method is the same for automatic or manual antisiphon valves. Antisiphon valves are the most common control valves, and many municipal codes require them. They must be raised above ground on risers to a height of 6 inches (or more if required by local codes). Space them 5 inches apart in the manifold for easy assembly and maintenance and at least that far from the house.

To assemble a series of antisiphon valves into a manifold, turn off the main irrigation shutoff valve and assemble the required number of manifold tees, 5 inches or more apart, using short sections of PVC pipe or special manifold pipe. Add a cap at the last tee of each manifold. This cap allows you to easily add more valves if needed. In freezing areas, add a manual drain valve instead of a cap to facilitate drainage.

Next, add an appropriate length of threaded PVC riser (remember, the antisiphon valve must be at least 6 inches higher than the highest head in the yard) to each manifold tee, then attach an antisiphon valve to each riser. Some antisiphon valves

INSTALLING PIPE, ELBOWS, AND TEES

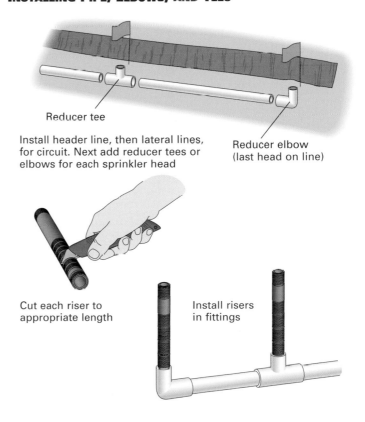

Reducer tee

Install header line, then lateral lines, for circuit. Next add reducer tees or elbows for each sprinkler head

Reducer elbow (last head on line)

Cut each riser to appropriate length

Install risers in fittings

PUTTING IT ALL TOGETHER
continued

TWO USES FOR FLEXIBLE RISER PIPE (SWING PIPE)

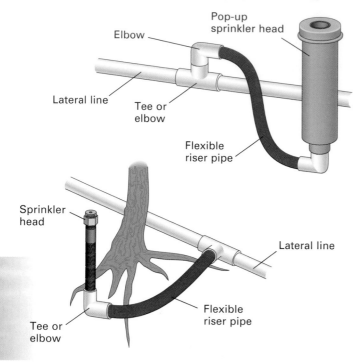

Pop-up
sprinkler head

Elbow

Lateral line

Tee or
elbow

Flexible
riser pipe

Sprinkler
head

Lateral line

Tee or
elbow

Flexible
riser pipe

require an adapter. Add another section of riser down from the valve to the bottom of the trench, then an elbow to direct the header pipe on its planned path. Turn off the control valves and turn on the water in the entire system to check for leaks, then open the control valves to flush out any dirt.

Do not install a valve of any kind, automatic or manual, downstream from an antisiphon valve or its antisiphon function will not work.

■ INSTALLING IN-LINE OR MANUAL ANGLE VALVES: If you use an unregulated water supply such as a well or tank, or if the local code requires a separate backflow prevention device, use either automatic in-line valves or manual angle valves. They are installed in manifolds in the same manner as antisiphon valves, but are usually placed underground in an inground valve box over a bed of gravel.

■ WIRING AUTOMATIC EQUIPMENT: Use 18-gauge wire approved for underground burial to attach automatic control valves to the controller. Bury the wire in trenches at least 6 inches deep. See "Using Your System," page 78, for further instructions for installing automatic equipment.

LAYING THE PIPE: Until this point, you've been using PVC pipe (or metal pipe if required by local codes) to protect the system from damage due to pressure surges. After the installation of the control valves, however, using flexible poly pipe becomes feasible. See "Choosing Piping Materials," page 40, for help deciding whether to do so. To connect poly pipe to PVC, insert the end of the pipe over the ridges of a PVC-to-poly adapter and tighten a stainless steel clamp over the pipe.

If you are using a trencher or pipe puller, dig all trenches at this stage. Otherwise, you may want to assemble each circuit first, hook it up to its control valve, and test it before digging the trenches. Start by installing the header line from the manifold to the end of its path, then attach the lateral lines—the ones to which the sprinkler heads will actually be connected—to the header line. Make all connections with appropriate elbows and tees.

ATTACHING RISERS AND SPRINKLER HEADS: Insert a reducer tee for each sprinkler head (substitute a reducer elbow for the last head on each line). Next, add a riser to each tee. Adjustable risers, although more expensive, are a good choice, as soil builds up in lawns and gardens over time and, when this happens, the risers can simply be twisted slightly to extend their length. Use a flexible riser or swing joint in zones of heavy traffic. Make sure each riser is vertical (except on slopes), and cut it to the appropriate height using a hacksaw. Stationary and pop-up lawn sprinkler

INSTALLING AUTOMATIC IN-LINE VALVES IN A MANIFOLD

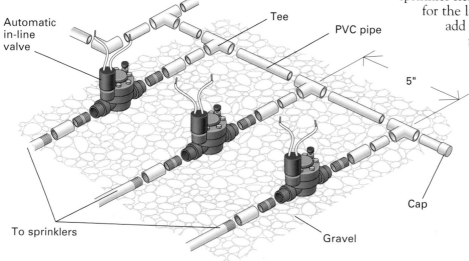

Automatic
in-line
valve

Tee

PVC pipe

5"

Cap

To sprinklers

Gravel

Cutting 2-inch-thick blocks of sod with a square-bladed shovel makes the sod easy to replace.

PROPER PLACING OF HEADS ON SLOPES

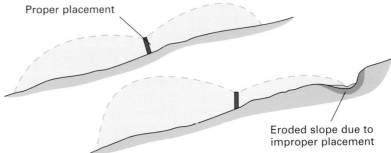

Proper placement

Eroded slope due to improper placement

heads should be within 1 inch of the soil, allowing room for the grass to grow and establish itself. Mount shrub heads as high as the expected maximum height of the plantings in that sector.

A depth of 6 inches is usually sufficient for sprinkler trenches, but extrahigh pop-up heads might require greater depth. Seal each riser, except the one at the end of the circuit, with a pipe plug and flush the system until the water runs clean. Next, turn off the water, remove the plugs from each riser, and flush again. Turn off the water when finished.

Install the appropriate sprinkler on each riser. Applying pipe joint tape or paste around the riser head will offer extra protection against leaks. Tie the riser to the stake or flag to keep it vertical.

CHECKING AND ADJUSTING THE CIRCUIT: Turn off any water running in the house and turn on the water in the circuit being installed. Check for leaks, then adjust for proper coverage. Starting with the sprinkler closest to the control valve, adjust its flow with a screwdriver (some rotary heads have a a flap to adjust). Next, redirect any part-circle spray patterns as needed. Impact heads have friction collars at the base of the nozzle for this purpose. A special key or ratchet (supplied by the manufacturer) is often needed to adjust the pattern of rotary heads. Repeat for each head. If there are spots not being properly watered, make adjustments. This may involve using different heads, respacing heads, adding heads, or moving a head from one circuit to another.

FINISHING THE JOB: Once you have tested each circuit, dig its trenches (if this has not already been done). If the soil is rocky or the trench bottom irregular, fill in with sand;

INSTALLATION ON SLOPES

There are two rules for installing sprinklers on slopes. First, because sprinkler heads will not water in a perfect circle (gravity will cause the throw radius in the lower sector to lengthen, and that in the upper sector to shorten), you must place the heads closer to the uphill side of the slope to maintain a proper spacing pattern. Second, always align sprinkler heads perpendicular to the slope, to prevent erosion on the uphill side.

moisten it and tamp it down. Lay the piping at the correct depth. At the base of each automatic drain valve or self-draining header, remove 6 inches of sand and soil and replace it with gravel; pack it down well. Repeat with the next circuit.

At day's end and after PVC pipe has set for at least 12 hours, fill in the trenches. First cover the pipes with a layer of sand to prevent damage when the soil is compacted, then backfill with soil.

In lawn areas, carefully tamp the sod back in place. You are now ready to water one entire sector with your new irrigation system.

INSTALLING SPRINKLERS ON RISERS

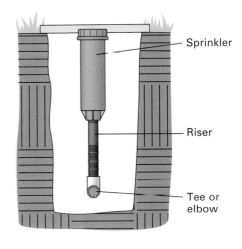

Sprinkler

Riser

Tee or elbow

Micro-irrigation allows you to distribute water only to the areas that need it, without wasting it on paths, paved areas, or plants that may not require as much as others. Here, micro-sprinklers on automatic timers keep plants in the raised beds green and lush.

MICRO-IRRIGATION

Micro-irrigation, or low-pressure irrigation, has long been considered the wave of the future. In fact, the future is already here. Micro-irrigation is now widely used in home systems of all kinds. Irrigation specialists include micro-irrigation in their projects as a matter of course, either in combination with sprinkler irrigation or on its own, and so can you. Setting up micro-irrigation can be as simple as running a porous hose through the garden and turning on the water, or it can involve the same precise planning, trenching, and piping necessary for a sprinkler system. This chapter presents the different possibilities so you can decide whether micro-irrigation is appropriate for your garden and, if so, what kind. You will also see several different ways of installing micro-irrigation, ranging from the simple to the complex.

THE BASICS OF MICRO-IRRIGATION

M icro-irrigation is an increasingly popular choice in landscaping. It is inexpensive, easy to install, and adaptable to many uses. It may be just the system you need.

HOW IT WORKS

Micro-sprinklers have a range of 6 to 11 feet.

If this book had been written a few years earlier, this chapter would have been called "Drip Irrigation," because most low-pressure irrigation systems watered plants drop by drop. Now low-pressure irrigation systems spray and mist as well as drip, so *micro-irrigation* is a more appropriate term. *Drip irrigation* is still used in the field, however.

Although sprinkler and micro-irrigation systems seem to have much in common, they are actually quite different. Sprinklers deliver a lot of water quickly and are designed for a drench-and-let-dry cycle. Sometimes much of the water drains away unused because it was applied too quickly for the soil and the plants to absorb it.

Micro-irrigation, on the other hand, keeps the root zone evenly moist at all times yet never so wet that the plants become waterlogged and subject to rot. It delivers small amounts of water more often and over a longer period of time. Typically, micro-irrigation emitters supply ½ to 2 gallons of water per hour (gph)—quite a contrast with sprinklers, whose flow is calculated in gallons per minute. No effort is made to soak the entire area from above. When applied slowly, water spreads laterally underground. You simply place emitters close enough together so their coverage zones meet.

Given its low flow rate, micro-irrigation doesn't require high water pressure. In fact, most systems must operate under low pressure. That's good news if the local system suffers bouts of low pressure, but most people will have to reduce the pressure coming from their supply line. This can be done by installing a pressure reducer at the beginning of the system, by using pressure-compensating emitters, or by combining the two.

RECENT DEVELOPMENTS

Clogged emitters were once a serious concern because so little water flows from their narrow outlets that flushing them is next to impossible. Most modern emitters, however, use a turbulent-flow design that keeps dirt particles in continuous motion so they can't settle until they leave the emitter. Modern emitters also reduce the speed of flow so water can flow drop by drop from a larger opening less subject to clogging.

Older emitters exposed to the sun's ultraviolet rays eventually became brittle and broke. Newer plastics don't have that problem. One problem remains: many micro-irrigation emitters are small and project from the ground, leaving them susceptible to foot traffic. The aboveground parts of micro-irrigation systems require the same careful placement as those of sprinkler components (see "Safety Considerations," page 35), and they must never be installed in lawns or where a lawn mower might hit them.

ZONES OF IRRIGATION JOINED UNDERGROUND

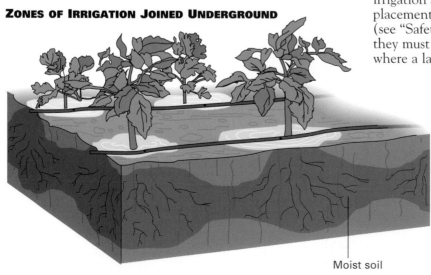

Moist soil

SELECTING COMPONENTS

Micro-irrigation offers an even wider variety of components than does high-pressure irrigation. Here are the elements you need to look at before you begin to plan a micro-irrigation system.

CHOOSING THE WHOLE ENSEMBLE

The choices in micro-irrigation are bewildering. Each company supplies a full range of drip emitters, sprinklers, misters, porous pipe, and in-line emitters, not to mention pipes, stakes, and fittings. Often these parts, though they look alike, are not compatible. For example, most irrigation parts are now color-coded to make replacing them easier; yet different manufacturers don't necessarily use the same color codes. Purchase all components from the same manufacturer.

PIPES

The choice is easy here: Micro-irrigation systems all use ½-inch polyethylene landscape pipe for at least the supply and header lines and sometimes all the lines, with ¼-inch or, more rarely, ⅛-inch vinyl tubing (spaghetti tubing) serving for lead-in tubes and lateral lines, especially for container gardens and micro-sprinkler systems. To connect the supply line to the water system, elementary aboveground drip systems often use garden hose, but more permanent situations generally use buried PVC or poly pipe for the main line.

The array of products for micro-irrigation is even greater than for sprinkler systems. Piping includes ½-inch poly pipe and ¼-inch vinyl tubing.

EMITTERS

There are four categories of emitters: porous pipe, punch-in emitters, emitter lines, and micro-sprinkler heads.

POROUS PIPE: Porous pipe is the easiest and least expensive irrigation option. Snake it around plantings, hook it up to an existing hose, and turn it on. Hide it with a bit of mulch. Generally made of recycled tires, it oozes water from tiny pores. How far the water travels horizontally varies according to your conditions, so do some tests before deciding on the permanent location of the pipe. Of course, it

Porous pipe emits water from tiny pores irregularly spaced along its entire surface.

SELECTING COMPONENTS
continued

SOIL TYPE VERSUS EMITTER FLOW RATE

Soil Type	Emitter Flow Rate
Clay soil	½ gph
Loam soil	1 gph
Sandy soil	2 gph

Emitters come in a wide range of shapes and capacities.

doesn't have to have a permanent location. Simply pick up porous pipe and move it as needed. On the other extreme, it can be buried 2 to 6 inches deep and become part of a permanent system. Porous pipe can be cut into sections and placed in lateral lines to give coverage similar to that of poly pipe.

On the negative side, due to the numerous pores situated irregularly over the entire surface, inner water pressure control is not possible. As a result, porous pipe waters unevenly, losing pressure toward the end of each length and overwatering low parts of its run while letting higher ones dry out. It can

therefore be used efficiently only on flat ground. It is especially important to use a fine filter (about 200 mesh), because the pores are easily clogged. Also, because the fittings for porous pipe tend to come apart under even moderate pressure, a special pressure regulator must be used to keep the circuit below 10 psi at all times.

Porous pipe is most often used in flower beds and vegetable gardens, under hedges, around large trees, and in mass plantings of shrubs—areas where its slightly uneven water delivery will not cause problems.

PUNCH-IN EMITTERS: These water outlets can be inserted directly into pipe after you punch a hole into it. They have an inlet barb at their base so that they won't pop back out. They can be installed anywhere along ½-inch poly pipe; simply make a hole with a hole punch and put one in. Or, they can be inserted in the end sections of ¼-inch or ⅛-inch tubing. Some emitters have self-piercing inlet barbs to punch their own holes. Just push and twist, and they're in.

Emitters come in regular and pressure-compensating forms. The latter are the better choice. They give off the same amount of water throughout the circuit even when there is a major difference in elevation or the tubing is particularly long.

Punch-in emitters have different flow rates, usually ½, 1, 2, and sometimes 4 gallons per hour. In general, use ½-gph emitters for clay soils, 1-gph emitters for loam soils, and 2-gph emitters for sandy soils. If you are unsure of your soil type, see "Types of Topsoil," page 14, or use 1-gph emitters. If you can see that some emitters in your system are not supplying enough water, simply replace them with those that are one flow rate higher, or add more emitters. If some sectors

Staking emitters ensures steady dripping.

get too much water, replace the emitters with those of a lower flow rate, or remove one or two emitters and plug the resulting holes.

The three main types of punch-in emitters are drip emitters, misters, and in-line drip emitters.

■ DRIP EMITTERS: The most popular punch-in emitters, these are suitable for containers, vegetable gardens, flower gardens, trees, and shrubs. They make up the foundation of drip irrigation, literally delivering water drop by drop and keeping the surface of the soil almost dry while keeping roots moist. They can be punched into ½-inch pipe laid on the ground or inserted into the ends of ¼-inch or ⅛-inch tubing and held off the ground by stakes. Some manufacturers produce drip emitters incorporated into stakes.

■ MISTERS: These are most popular in greenhouses and with specialists who grow high-humidity plants such as ferns and bromeliads. Otherwise they are used only in very dry climates to keep fine-leaved annuals, perennials, and tropicals in top shape. In less arid climates, they are sometimes used to humidify hanging baskets. Most give off a fine mist that humidifies the air but rarely collects on the leaves. Those designed to give larger water droplets serve a double purpose: They moisten the air, and the droplets that form drip down to the base of the plant to water its roots. Because misters must be run at regular intervals during the day, but only for a few minutes at a time, they should be on a different circuit than any other emitter and preferably on a controller.

Misters must be attached to their pot using a clip or stake; each manufacturer has its own device. Some misters can be, or already are, incorporated into a special combination stake that can be inserted into potting soil or nailed or screwed to an outside support.

■ IN-LINE DRIP EMITTERS: These emitters are a hybrid between a drip emitter and an emitter line. Like punch-in emitters, they are inserted individually into the water line according to need. Like emitter lines, however, they fit right into the line and not on its periphery. Water simply flows through them and continues on, allowing some water to drip out as it passes. In-line emitters are simple to install. Cut the tubing wherever water is needed, insert the barbed ends into the cut section of the tube, and push back together. Most are designed for ¼-inch tubing only. They have a more limited range of flow rates than do drip emitters, usually only ½ or 1 gph. In-line

emitters are used mostly in flower boxes and vegetable gardens because they are most efficient at watering small plants in short rows.

EMITTER LINES: True emitter lines incorporate equally spaced emitters directly into ½-inch pipe. As water runs through the line, some drips out. The emitters come preinstalled at 12-, 18-, 24-, and 36-inch spacings and are rated to dispense ½ or 1 gph of water. Lines with ½-gph emitters are used for clay soils, lines with 1-gph emitters for loam soils, and lines with 2-gph emitters for sandy soils.

All emitter lines have the turbulent-flow design to keep them from clogging. In most cases, especially on a long line or on a steep slope, use pressure-compensating emitter lines.

Sold in rolls, emitter lines can be cut to length and connected to the main line or other laterals in the same way as any other poly pipe. These practical and durable watering devices might be hard to find but are worth looking for because they give excellent results in flower beds and vegetable gardens, under hedges, around large trees, and in mass plantings of shrubs. They are simply laid on the ground and covered with mulch. They are also much less subject to breakage than punch-in emitters because the emitters are actually part of the pipe and they can't accidentally be pulled apart. On the down side, the regularly spaced emitters don't allow as much flexibility as individual emitters do. Emitter lines are most practical where groupings of similar plants are evenly spaced.

MICRO-SPRINKLER HEADS: Also called low-volume sprayers, micro-sprinkler heads take their place between micro-irrigation and sprinkler irrigation, right where the differences begin to dissolve. These mini-sprinklers, in fact, are the main reason why the term *drip irrigation* is no longer entirely

TWO TYPES OF IN-LINE EMITTERS

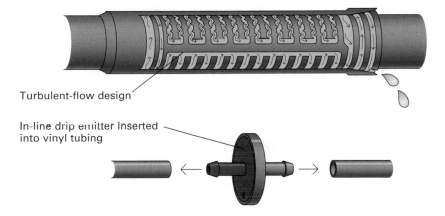

Turbulent-flow design

In-line drip emitter Inserted into vinyl tubing

SELECTING COMPONENTS
continued

A SELECTION OF MICRO-SPRINKLER HEADS

appropriate. Micro-sprinkler heads use low water pressure and narrow-diameter pipes as drip systems do, yet apply water in a fanlike spray as sprinklers do. They are not as efficient as punch-in and in-line micro-irrigation, since they lose some water to evaporation; yet they waste less water than high-pressure sprinklers.

You can think of micro-sprinkler heads as less powerful relatives of high-pressure heads. They can spray in full circles or increments of a circle, even in strips. Most cover a radius of 6 to 11 feet and are ideal for small beds. They are usually set in beds on tubelike risers and don't retract into the ground after use. With careful placement, they are relatively inconspicuous because they are so narrow. These heads are most popular in flower beds, mass plantings, and ground covers. Because they don't retract and have restricted range, they can't be used on lawns other than as incidental sprayers in areas of overlap.

Micro-bubblers are based on the same principle as micro-sprinkler heads. They are used primarily for shrub plantings, but also work in flower beds and ground covers.

CONVERTING TO MICRO-IRRIGATION

If you already have a sprinkler system, it is often possible to convert everything but lawn areas to micro-irrigation without digging or removing pipes—just buy a converter or retrofit kit. These kits allow you to convert a single spray head to single or multiple micro-irrigation watering devices.

However, entire circuits must be converted. It is not possible to have a circuit that contains both high-pressure sprinklers and low-pressure micro-irrigation.

First turn off the water at the main sprinkler shutoff valve and twist off the old sprinkler head to reveal the riser. Turn on the circuit to flush out any sediment. Install on the riser the appropriate adapter for the kind of converter kit you have chosen, plus the converter itself. Single-outlet emission devices permit you to convert one sprinkler head to a single micro-irrigation device. Multi-outlet emission devices allow you to add, for each original sprinkler head, six or more outlets for an equivalent number of lengths of ¼-inch poly tubing can be added to direct the drip-irrigation flow in any direction. If all outlets are not needed immediately (as is often the case), don't remove the plugs from the unneeded ones; keep them for future use. For exact installation details, simply follow the manufacturer's instructions.

In the case of pop-up sprinklers where the riser is underground beneath the housing and hard to reach, it is often easier to use the housing as an adapter than to remove it. Many suppliers offer a retrofit kit designed for this purpose. These kits are not universal, however. Make sure that the kit you choose is adapted to the sprinkler line. To install, remove the nozzle mechanism of the pop-up sprinkler from the housing and insert the retrofit kit: a pressure regulator, filter, and section of threaded riser. Attach the micro-irrigation device of your choice to the top of the riser.

The conversion process will leave you with a number of unused spray heads that must be capped. To do so, add a ½-inch threaded cap to each unused riser. Special caps are also available to cover unused pop-up sprinkler housings.

SIZING THE MICRO-IRRIGATION SYSTEM

Drawing a plot map for micro-irrigation is similar to doing a sprinkler system plan (see page 42). To the plan you have drawn of your property, just add the required micro-irrigation circuits. Keep the manufacturer's equipment chart handy.

Micro-sprinkler heads can be plotted in the same way as high-pressure sprinkler heads are; you just draw smaller circles of coverage (see page 42). For all other low-pressure emitter devices, just plot the lines.

PLOTTING MASS PLANTINGS

Micro-irrigation pipe is generally laid out as a series of relatively parallel lateral lines that eventually form a rectangular shape. Using parallel lines set 12 to 24 inches apart (that is, at distances where two water spreads meet) is the most efficient way to ensure even watering. In general, set the lines closer (12 inches) in sandy soils, farther apart (18 to 24 inches) in loam or clay soils.

Connect parallel lateral lines to a single ½-inch supply line, called the header line, which connects back to the main supply line. Do not add emitters to the header or main supply lines. Connect the supply and lateral lines using tees and elbows.

The end of each lateral line must be closed off. This is done with an end closure (see page 72). Each line can terminate with its own end closure, or you can close the rectangle by adding another piece of supply line that leads to a single end closure per circuit. The latter option takes more effort to install, but is less work in the long run because micro-irrigation lines must be drained periodically, and it is easier to remove two or three end closures than several dozen.

For areas watered by parallel lateral lines, you can use punch-in emitters and emitter lines interchangeably. Porous pipe can be substituted as long as you take its slightly irregular water delivery into account. Some manufacturers suggest ¼-inch vinyl tubing with in-line drip emitters for areas where short lateral lines are needed, but such tubing is more delicate to work with than standard ½-inch poly pipe and is best restricted to hanging baskets and containers, where thicker pipe is undesirable.

PLOTTING ISOLATED PLANTINGS

It is inefficient to water isolated or well-spaced plants, such as trees, using parallel line irrigation—you'd have more pipe than emitters. Instead, run a single ½-inch supply line to within the drip line of the plant. If there are several well-spaced plants in the

MICRO-IRRIGATION PLAN

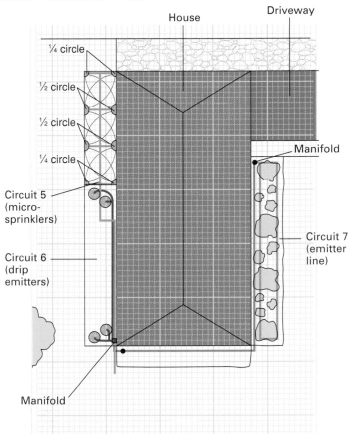

PARALLEL DRIP LINES WITH TWO TYPES OF END CLOSURE

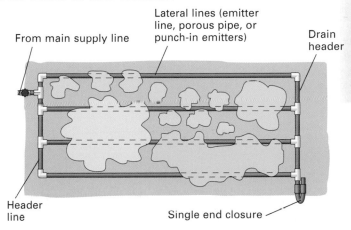

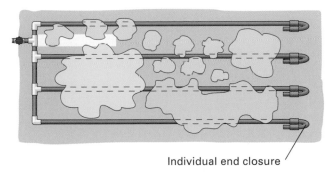

Individual end closure

SIZING THE MICRO-IRRIGATION SYSTEM
continued

IRRIGATING ISOLATED PLANTINGS

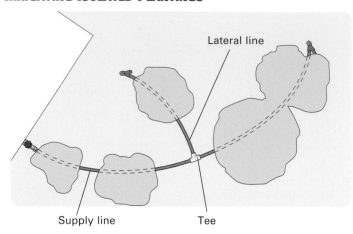

Lateral line

Supply line   Tee

THREE EMITTER SETUPS

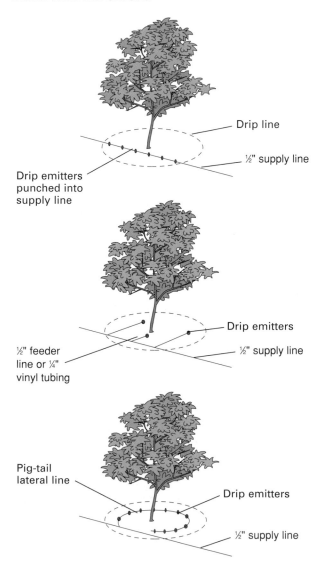

Drip line

½" supply line

Drip emitters
punched into
supply line

Drip emitters

½" feeder
line or ¼"
vinyl tubing

½" supply line

Pig-tail
lateral line

Drip emitters

½" supply line

NUMBER OF EMITTERS PER PLANT BASED ON CANOPY DIAMETER	
Plant Canopy Diameter	**Emitters per Plant**
Up to 3'	1
3–5'	2
6–9'	3
10' and more	1 per 2½ feet of canopy diameter

vicinity, snake the supply line toward each, or use tee connectors to attach additional lateral lines. There is no need to use straight lines because poly pipe is flexible.

Isolated plants will absorb water from anywhere within their root area, but, for more efficient results, place emitters or an emitter line a few inches from the base of smaller plants and at about one-third to one-half the distance away from the center of the foliage canopy for larger plants. The chart above will help you determine the number of emitters needed. Watch the plant over time and adjust the number or size of emitters as needed.

For example, a small shrub needs only one emitter, but a tree with a 15-foot canopy requires six (15 divided by 2½). Use the chart on page 71 to determine the flow rate of the emitters required.

There are several ways to water a plant once the pipe has reached it.
■ Punch emitters directly into the line.
■ Use a short section of line as a feeder line leading from the supply line to within the plant's canopy, and add emitters. Use either ½-inch poly pipe or ¼-inch vinyl.
■ For plants where four or more emitters will be needed, loop a short section of line around the plant and attach it to the supply line with a tee connector. This is called a pigtail. You can use emitter line, porous pipe, or plain ½-inch poly pipe and emitters.

After placing the pipe, flush it. Then plug the end of the supply line and any laterals.

In many cases, you'll want to bury the supply line. If so, check municipal regulations, particularly any concerning backflow prevention. Do not bury emitters or emitter line; cover them with mulch instead.

DIVIDING INTO CIRCUITS

Divide the system into circuits according to the needs of the plants. This is easier than with sprinkler irrigation because you can adjust for localized watering needs by adding or removing emitters or changing their sizes. You can easily combine shrubs, trees, ground covers, and flower beds on the same circuit. The main determining factors for dividing micro-irrigation into circuits are maximum line length and number of emitters required.

Almost all emitters are now pressure-compensating, meaning that zones of higher or lower elevation will receive equal amounts of water and can be combined. This, plus the fact that you can use enormously long pipe (each line can hold hundreds of emitters), means you can often group all the inground ornamental plants of a small to medium yard in one circuit. Vegetable beds should, however, be on a separate circuit due to their more seasonal use, as should container plants, which often require daily watering. Misters should be on a separate circuit.

■ LINE LENGTH: The basic guideline for plain poly pipe or porous pipe is to use no more than 200 feet in a single circuit.

The length of pressure-compensating emitter line per circuit varies considerably depending on the spacing of the emitters and their flow rate, but can range from 326 feet for ½ gph emitter line on 12-inch centers to 248 feet for 1 gph emitter line on 12-inch centers. As the spacing increases, so does the length of emitter line that can be used. For emitter line on 24-inch centers, the usable length per circuit jumps to 584 feet for ½ gph emitter line and 444 feet for ½ gph emitter line. These numbers may vary. Consult the manufacturer's recommendations. Use much shorter lengths of ¼-inch vinyl tubing.

■ NUMBER OF EMITTERS: Like line length, the total gallonage per circuit is limited; it should not be more than 150 gph. Therefore, you need to total up the gph of the emitters for each proposed circuit to make sure they fall within the accepted maximum. There is plenty of leeway. You could use up to 300 ½ gph emitters (300 × ½), 150 1 gph emitters (150 × 1), or 75 2 gph emitters (75 × 2) per circuit.

Micro-sprinklers are an exception. Their water use resembles that of sprinklers more than that of other emitters. They must always be on a separate circuit from other micro-irrigation devices because of their greater water use. The flow rate of a micro-sprinkler varies from 7 to 25 gph, compared to only ½ to 2 gph for most emitters. Therefore, you cannot use as many micro-sprinklers per

IRRIGATING A FLOWER BED

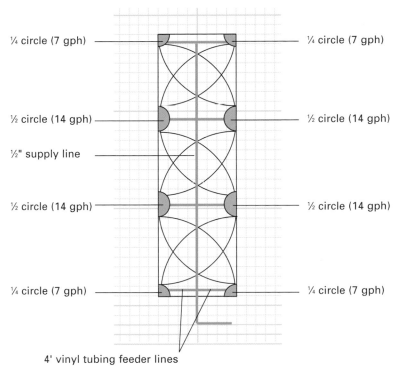

¼ circle (7 gph)
¼ circle (7 gph)
½ circle (14 gph)
½ circle (14 gph)
½" supply line
½ circle (14 gph)
½ circle (14 gph)
¼ circle (7 gph)
¼ circle (7 gph)

4' vinyl tubing feeder lines

circuit as emitters and you probably will have to divide large micro-sprinkler zones into more than one circuit. Take these factors into account:

■ The radius of a micro-sprinkler, like that of a high-pressure sprinkler, should always overlap its neighbor's. Since there is little wind drift, the minimum overlap is only 25 percent of the diameter.

■ Many micro-sprinklers require a minimum water pressure of 20 or 25 psi.

■ Don't use more than 150 feet of ½-inch poly pipe per circuit.

■ The gallonage per circuit shouldn't exceed 200 gph.

■ Use no more than 5 feet of ¼-inch vinyl tubing between the ½-inch supply pipe and a full-circle sprinkler, or 10 feet for half-circle, quarter-circle, or strip sprinklers.

Micro-sprinklers vary in flow rates, so always check the manufacturer's specifications. For example, one manufacturer rates its full-circle micro-sprinklers at 25 gph, its half circles at 14 gph, and its quarter circles at 7 gph. One possible circuit that would remain under the 200 gph limit would be four quarter-circle micro-sprinklers, five half circles, and four full circles: *(4 × 7) + (5 × 14) + (4 × 25) = 198 gph.*

INSTALLING MICRO-IRRIGATION

If you are looking for a quick, easy, and inexpensive watering system and don't mind a few pipes in the landscape, follow the recommendations in "Surface Installation," at right. If you want the system to be as permanent and integrated into the landscape as most sprinkler systems are, see "Subsurface Supply-Line Installation," page 70. You can also combine the two, putting parts such as supply lines, underground and others, such as lateral lines, aboveground.

LOCATING SHUTOFF VALVES

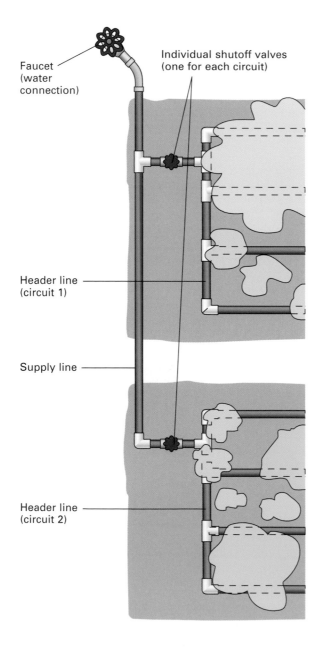

Faucet (water connection)

Individual shutoff valves (one for each circuit)

Header line (circuit 1)

Supply line

Header line (circuit 2)

Surface installation does not require trenching and is so simple you can have an entire circuit up and running in one afternoon. By not burying the pipe, you avoid many of the usual municipal-code restrictions on location of a system and materials. On the other hand, it is important to plan carefully so the exposed pipe is not too visible and runs through areas where there is no foot traffic. Often this means you'll be running pipe in at least two sections: one line around the house to water foundation plantings and other nearby beds, and another line around the periphery of the lot to reach trees and shrubs planted there.

Because surface installations are often manual and connected to faucets, that type of hookup is discussed here. However, you can make a surface system automatic or hook it up as you would a subsurface installation (see page 70).

CONNECTING TO A FAUCET: A proper faucet connection uses a series of connected valves that, in concert, control the system's water pressure, filtering, and backflow prevention. If there are several outdoor faucets, it might be possible for each to supply one or two circuits that are turned off and on at the faucet. Usually, though, a single supply line is installed that leads from the water connection. Individual circuits are then turned on and off by shutoff valves located at the head of each circuit. This reduces the octopuslike assembly of pipes running from a single faucet.

Start with a dual shutoff Y-connector, with one outlet attached to the water connection and the other outlet left available. This is especially wise if the yard has only one outdoor faucet. If a second outdoor faucet is available, you could reserve it entirely for irrigation. Use the Y-connector to assemble a second water connector for another part of the irrigation system, forming a simple two-circuit manifold.

Next you'll need a backflow preventer. This is essential even if your municipal code does not mention it. For surface irrigation systems, a simple faucet-type antisiphon vacuum breaker is sufficient unless the local code states otherwise. For a more detailed discussion, see "Preventing Backflow," page 48.

The filter is next in line. Some so-called complete micro-irrigation kits don't include one, but a filter is essential because the emitter outlets are so narrow that even the modern turbulent-flow emitters can be clogged by a few flakes of rust or other debris. Y-filters are the best choice, since they are both efficient and easy to clean. If you're on a well system that might pick up sand, look for a sand-type Y-filter. T-filters can also be used.

The pressure regulator comes next. Although some manufacturers of pressure-compensating emitters and emitter lines claim their micro-irrigation products can run at normal water pressure, it would be unfortunate to see the system blow apart if the pressure rose to abnormal levels. A pressure regulator will prevent that and also prolong the life of pipes and emitters by ensuring constant low pressure. The simplest pressure-regulation device is the pressure-compensating flow control, which looks like a tiny washer. Better known and more efficient are preset pressure regulators. Buy one appropriate to the needs of the emitters you'll be using: 15, 20, 25, and 30 psi are the most common. Be sure to install pressure regulators the right direction; most casings have a stamped arrow indicating the direction of flow. Point the arrow in the direction of the irrigation system, not the house.

Because all the elements of the water connection are designed for ¾-inch or 1-inch connections, finish with an adapter called a line connection, into which you can insert ½-inch solid supply pipe.

As you assemble the elements of a water connection, add Teflon tape or paste to each threaded fitting to ensure a good seal. You may also need one or two hose-to-thread adapters. (Iron pipe threads are more closely spaced than hose threads are, so trying to twist one onto the other could ruin both.) You might also encounter instances in which two devices meant to fit together in the series both have either male or female threads. If so, use an adapter.

Finish the water connection by solidifying it, if necessary, with metal or wooden stakes, and placing a 4- to 6-inch layer of gravel under its base to help absorb water resulting from flushing the filter.

INSTALLING SUPPLY LINES:
Stake out the yard according to the plan, then lay out the main supply line from the water connection to the head of each circuit. The line will be less stiff and easier to manage if you let it sit in the sun first, but you'll still probably need to hold it in place

with a few wire stakes. Never stretch exposed poly pipe so it is completely taut. Leave room for expansion and contraction, especially in cold climates.

Poly pipe can be assembled using couplings, tees, or elbows (see "Working With Poly Pipe," page 51). Unlike ¾-inch or larger pipe, ½-inch poly pipe often uses compression fittings instead of ridged insert fittings with clamps. With insert fittings, the fitting is inserted into the pipe; with compression fittings, the pipe is inserted into the fitting. Simply push and twist until the pipe is inserted about 1 inch into the fitting; soak the end of the pipe in warm water first if it is too stiff. The fitting will cling to the poly pipe by compression, forming a perfect seal.

Begin assembling the supply lines. To link sections of pipe together, or at points where the main supply line branches or abruptly turns a corner, add a tee, elbow, or coupling. When you come to the head of a new circuit, add a manual shutoff valve (a ball valve, for

TYPICAL FAUCET CONNECTION ASSEMBLY

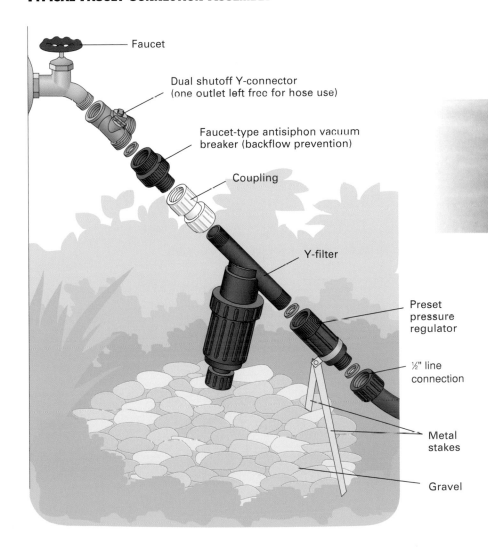

Faucet

Dual shutoff Y-connector (one outlet left free for hose use)

Faucet-type antisiphon vacuum breaker (backflow prevention)

Coupling

Y-filter

Preset pressure regulator

½" line connection

Metal stakes

Gravel

INSTALLING MICRO-IRRIGATION
continued

COMPRESSION FITTINGS

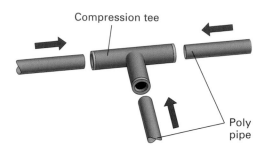

Compression tee

Poly pipe

INSTALLING LATERAL LINES

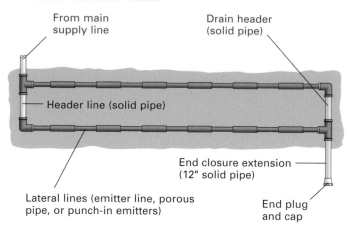

From main supply line

Drain header (solid pipe)

Header line (solid pipe)

End closure extension (12" solid pipe)

Lateral lines (emitter line, porous pipe, or punch-in emitters)

End plug and cap

example). This allows you to turn each circuit on and off separately. The shutoff valves should not be inserted into the main supply line itself unless it is the last circuit on the line; instead, insert the valves into a secondary section of supply line, because each circuit must be turned on and off independently from the others.

From the shutoff valve, add supply line as needed to reach the spot where the header line will be placed. Now turn on the water and flush. You are ready to install the circuit. (See "Lateral-Lines Installation," page 71.)

SUBSURFACE SUPPLY-LINE INSTALLATION

This is the best option for an inconspicuous system because all supply pipe is safely underground. Subsurface irrigation systems will last longer and should be considered the only truly permanent micro-irrigation system.

BRINGING UNDERGROUND PIPE TO THE SURFACE

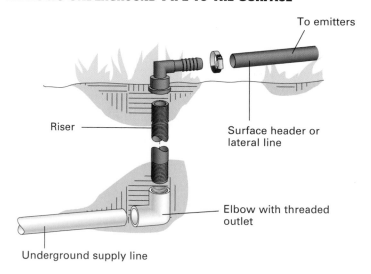

To emitters

Riser

Surface header or lateral line

Elbow with threaded outlet

Underground supply line

On the other hand, burying pipe means you'll have to investigate local codes, do a great deal of trenching, and spend longer doing the installation.

The installation of subsurface supply lines is similar to that described for sprinkler systems in the previous chapter. You have the same decisions to make in determining which valves you need, grouping them in manifolds, staking, and trenching. Micro-irrigation systems can share the same manifolds as sprinkler systems and the same controllers, as long as they are on separate circuits and have a pressure regulator. Although the two may be watering different sectors of the yard at different pressures, they are all part of the same system. As with sprinkler systems, either poly or PVC pipe can be used from the water connection to the head of the circuit.

Be aware that although a pressure regulator is not used in most sprinkler systems, it is essential to micro-irrigation. Its purpose and installation are described in "Connecting to a Faucet," page 68. It should be placed as the last element of the manifold, at a rate of one regulator per circuit.

Emitters are usually set aboveground, even in subsurface micro-irrigation. Only porous hose and treated emitter line are ever fully buried. Subsurface supply lines are set 8 to 12 inches deep. This means the supply line will have to be brought to the surface level again to join the header. To do this, use an elbow joint and a piece of PVC pipe or poly pipe acting as a riser.

With subsurface installation, 1-inch or ¾-inch PVC or poly pipe is commonly used for all underground sections up to the header lines, which are usually made of ½-inch poly pipe (sometimes PVC pipe). Use a reducing fitting to join the two sections. Finish by flushing well.

LATERAL-LINES INSTALLATION

CONTROL SYSTEM WITH PRESSURE REGULATOR

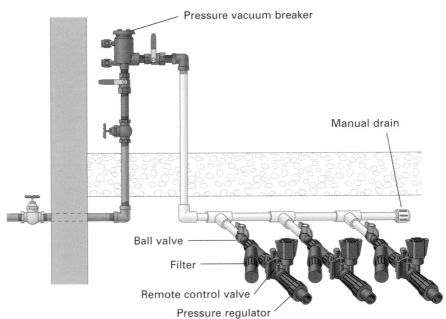

- Pressure vacuum breaker
- Manual drain
- Ball valve
- Filter
- Remote control valve
- Pressure regulator

From here on, micro-irrigation installation is the same whether you use surface or subsurface supply lines. Start off by staking out the positions of the header lines, drain lines, and lateral lines. Next, cut ½-inch poly pipe to the proper length and place it along the strings indicating its position.

INSTALLING PARALLEL LINES:

Header lines and drain lines require solid (unpierced) poly pipe. Some people prefer to use PVC pipe for both. Lateral lines, however, can be made of emitter line, porous pipe, or solid poly pipe to which you can then add emitters. Cut the header line as needed and insert tees or elbows where the laterals join it. If you've used compression fittings most commonly supplied with micro-irrigation kits, assemble by simultaneously pushing and twisting the pipe into the fitting. For instructions on installing other kinds of connectors, see "Working with Poly Pipe," page 51. Now connect the lateral lines to the header line and flush until the water runs clear.

Next, assemble the drain line at the opposite end of the laterals, in the same way as the header. Extend one line about 12 inches beyond the rectangle formed by the header and drainage lines for use as an end-closure extension. If you choose not to use a drain line, leave 12 inches of spare poly pipe at the end of each lateral line for end closure. Flush again.

Install an end closure at each unattached lateral line. Figure-8 end closures are popular. To install, insert the end closure over the pipe, then bend back the end of the pipe and insert it in the other opening of the figure 8, pinching off water circulation. A drawback of the figure 8 is that the bent section of the pipe may eventually crack. A hose end plug costs more, but is longer lasting. Insert the end of the lateral line into the compression fitting of the end plug. The cap can then be screwed on or off as needed. Always place end closures at the lowest part in the system.

At this point, drip emitters can be inserted into the lateral lines using a special hole punch. Formerly one emitter was placed at the base of each plant, but years of experience have shown that plants grow better when the entire root zone is kept evenly moist. to achieve this, space emitters regularly along the entire length of the lateral line rather than applying water to individual plants. Only where plants are spaced well apart should emitters be used at the rate of one per plant. The chart below gives suggestions for placement.

INSTALLING LINES FOR ISOLATED PLANTINGS:

Lay out the ½-inch poly pipe as determined in your plan (see Irrigating Isolated Plantings, page 66), starting with the supply line, then the laterals, and finally any feeder lines, using tees and elbows as needed to connect the lines. Pin them down with metal or wooden stakes, if necessary. Insert drip emitters within the lines as needed according to the explanations given on page

DRIP-EMITTER PLACEMENT

Soil Type	Emitter Flow	Plant Spacing	Preferred Emitter Placement
Clay	½ gph	Up to 24"	Every 24"
		25" or more	1 per plant*
Loam	1 gph	Up to 18"	Every 18"
		19" or more	1 per plant*
Sand	2 gph	Up to 12"	Every 12"
		3" or more	1 per plant*

*For small- and medium-sized plants. For shrubs, trees, and other large plants, see "Number of Emitters per Plant Based on Canopy Diameter," page 66.

INSTALLING MICRO-IRRIGATION
continued

66. Any sections that have no emitters can be buried 6 inches deep or more. Flush well. Terminate each unconnected line with an end closure.

INSTALLING MICRO-SPRINKLERS: Stake out the sectors to be watered using stakes or flags to represent the positions of the supply hose and the lateral lines. Assemble the sprinkler stakes. There is usually a thin riser that must be screwed or pressed into the top. Then sink them lightly into the soil to mark the planned positions of the sprinklers.

Lay out the ½-inch supply line and assemble it with connector tees and elbows. It should be no farther than 5 feet from full-circle micro-sprinkler heads or 10 feet from half, quarter, or strip heads, because those are the limits for ¼-inch vinyl tubing, given the relatively high gph needs of micro-sprinklers. Cut the vinyl tubing to the length needed to reach from the stake to a convenient point on the ½-inch supply line, leaving a few inches of slack for adjustments.

Now punch a hole in the supply line with a hole punch, insert a connector in one end of the vinyl tubing, and plug the connector into the supply line. Attach the other end of the tubing to the barbed connection on the stake. Some stakes include a clip or notch into which the tubing can be slipped to prevent it from being yanked off the stake.

Turn on the supply line and flush until clean. Cap it with an end closure. Insert the appropriate type of micro-sprinkler into the top of each riser. Turn on the water again, and adjust the location and

WORKING WITH VINYL TUBING AND POLY PIPE

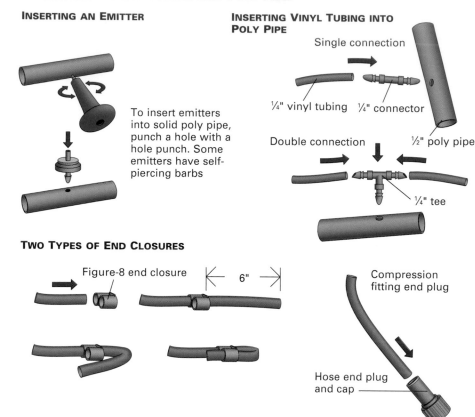

INSERTING AN EMITTER

To insert emitters into solid poly pipe, punch a hole with a hole punch. Some emitters have self-piercing barbs

INSERTING VINYL TUBING INTO POLY PIPE

Single connection

¼" vinyl tubing   ¼" connector

½" poly pipe

Double connection

¼" tee

TWO TYPES OF END CLOSURES

Figure-8 end closure   6"

Compression fitting end plug

Hose end plug and cap

TWO USES FOR ¼" VINYL TUBING

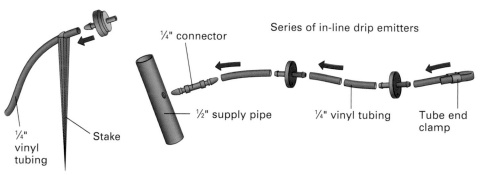

¼" connector

Series of in-line drip emitters

½" supply pipe   ¼" vinyl tubing   Tube end clamp

¼" vinyl tubing

Stake

Feeder line for individual drip emitters

REPAIRING BLUNDERS

It is all too easy to accidentally punch a hole in the wrong section of pipe or, after testing the circuits, to find one section that has too many emitters. This is easily corrected by cutting off the offending emitters and filling in the holes with hole plugs, often called goof plugs. Always have a few on hand when working with a hole punch.

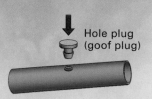

Hole plug (goof plug)

WORKING WITH VINYL TUBING

Inserting lengths of ¼- or ⅛-inch vinyl tubing as feeder line into ½-inch poly pipe is no more complicated than inserting a drip emitter. Just cut appropriate lengths of vinyl tubing with pruning shears or a knife, then punch a hole in the poly header pipe with a hole punch. Insert a barbed connector into the hole, then insert the other end of the barbed connector into the length of vinyl tubing. Where two sections of vinyl tubing must be attached at the same spot, used a barbed tee connector. If the vinyl tubing is too stiff, soak it in warm water before use. Do not use glue, oil, or lubricants to assemble the parts.

Each section of vinyl tubing can be connected to a single drip emitter or a series of in-line drip emitters. The ordinary drip emitter is simply inserted at the end of the section of tubing. The emitter should be held off the ground with a stake to keep it from clogging. In-line emitters are inserted by cutting the tubing at the appropriate spot, inserting the emitter, and pushing the tubing back into place around it.

Any section of tubing that does not end in a drip emitter should be plugged with a tube end clamp, which is used in much the same fashion as a figure-8 end clamp. Like all pipe, vinyl tubing must be flushed before installing end caps or terminal emitters.

To water trees or shrubs, space in-line drip emitters evenly along the line within the canopy area according to the number required (see chart on page 66). For other plants, refer to Drip Emitter Placement, page 71.

No more than 50 feet of ¼-inch tubing can be used in one circuit and no more than 25 feet as lateral line. (Use ⅛-inch tubing for only very short runs.) Likewise, vinyl tubing will support only a relatively small number of emitters—a total 15 gph. You could thus incorporate up to thirty ½-gph emitters or fifteen 1-gph emitters per circuit.

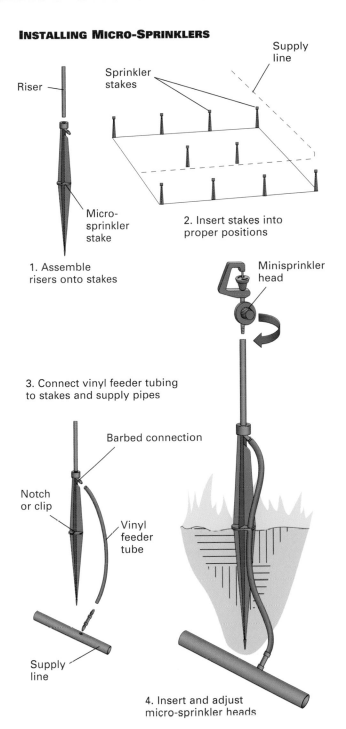

INSTALLING MICRO-SPRINKLERS

1. Assemble risers onto stakes

2. Insert stakes into proper positions

3. Connect vinyl feeder tubing to stakes and supply pipes

4. Insert and adjust micro-sprinkler heads

direction of the micro-sprinklers until you have complete coverage, then sink the stakes firmly into the ground. Depending on need, the supply line and lateral lines can be buried 4 to 6 inches below the ground or can be covered with mulch.

HIDING THE LINES: Once micro-irrigation is installed, the array of pipes can be unsightly, even if the nonemitting lines were buried. As plants grow, their foliage will help hide the lines, but in the meantime, you can mulch.

Decorative mulches do not block emitter outlets as soil can and therefore can be used to cover up emitter line, porous pipe, and any other landscape pipe that cannot be buried. Mulches come in a variety of textures, forms, and shades, from bark pieces to chopped cacao hulls to decorative stone. Mulches help decrease evaporation, thereby reducing watering needs, and encourage better plant growth. Don't apply so much mulch that it prevents micro-sprinklers and other sprayers from reaching their entire zone.

INSTALLING MICRO-IRRIGATION
continued

IRRIGATING A CONTAINER GARDEN UNOBTRUSIVELY

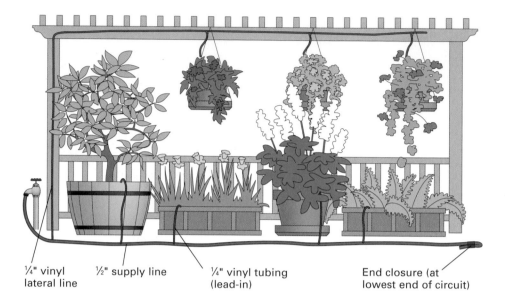

¼" vinyl lateral line

½" supply line

¼" vinyl tubing (lead-in)

End closure (at lowest end of circuit)

CONTAINER GARDENS: A SPECIAL CASE

Exposed to drying air and burning sun, container plants need more water more often than in-ground plants. Micro-irrigation is a perfect solution.

Drop by drop, day in and day out, automated micro-irrigation keeps the containers evenly moist. It is easily adapted to the plants' needs. If you like to move containers about, simply insert a hole plug in any unneeded tubing and punch into the supply line elsewhere.

Due to their special watering needs, container gardens should always be on their own circuits. In many cases, you'll be watering daily, instead of every two or three days, and for shorter periods than other gardens.

Generally speaking, one or two drip emitters per container are sufficient, although long flower boxes may require three or more, set at about 12-inch intervals. If misters are used, only one is needed per container. Low-flow (½-gph) emitters are preferred, so water is applied slowly to avoid overflow, and they should be pressure-compensating, especially if hanging baskets are used in the circuit.

Depending on conditions, micro-irrigation should be left on for an hour or two, the time needed to moisten the mix entirely. When water begins to run out of the drainage holes, turn off the system.

Micro-irrigation may be efficient, but without proper planning it is also visible. Try running the supply line along the periphery of the growing space and behind the pots or even under a wood patio. Vinyl tubing can be led up the back of the pots or even up through a drainage hole before being clamped into place with a small stake.

Rather than run a series of tubes up the back of the same container, use a section of ¼-inch tubing for a lead-in, then bend it into the pot with an elbow. Place the tubing around the inside of the pot and insert in-line drip emitters about every 12 inches. Plug the end of the tubing with a hole plug or by inserting a drip emitter.

Watering hanging baskets requires more care. Run the line up the supporting structure in the least obtrusive spot, then across the top. Use ¼-inch vinyl tubing if possible, because it is easier to hide. However, it cannot be used in more than 25-foot lengths (see "Working With Vinyl Tubing," page 73), so ½-inch poly tube may be required as a lateral line. Special support clamps for vinyl tubing and ½-inch pipe make it easy to fasten them, without crushing, to posts or masonry.

After installing micro-irrigation in containers, but before adding end-closure devices, turn on the water and flush the tubing thoroughly.

All container systems require adjustment over time. For one thing, as plants grow they require more water. You can leave the system on for a longer period, but that works only if the needs of all the containers increase at the same speed. Otherwise, replace selected emitters with ones that provide a greater flow rate, or add extra emitters.

Another change comes with the end of summer, when watering requirements are reduced. Turn on the system for shorter periods. If any containers still get too much water, clamp off tubing or remove emitters and plug the holes.

Finally, in areas with freezing temperatures, drain the irrigation system in the fall. If possible, disconnect it and bring it indoors for the winter.

NUMBER OF ½-GPH DRIP EMITTERS PER CONTAINER

Container Diameter	Number of Emitters
Up to 6"	1
7"–12"	2
13"–18"	3
19"–29"	4
Over 29"	1 every 6"

SPECIAL WATERING SITUATIONS FOR CONTAINERS

HANGING CONTAINER

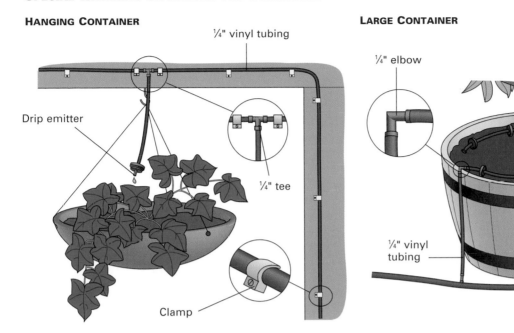

¼" vinyl tubing

Drip emitter

¼" tee

Clamp

LARGE CONTAINER

¼" elbow

In-line emitters

¼" vinyl tubing

Supply line

VEGETABLE GARDENS

Micro-irrigation is easily adaptable, so don't hesitate to use your ingenuity to find easy and practical solutions. Vegetable gardens are a good example, because their needs differ from those of other gardens in many respects. But don't throw away your hand sprinkler; newly seeded sections require hand watering until the seedlings are well established.

Vegetable gardens should be on a separate circuit where possible, because they need frequent, often daily, watering. Municipal regulations restricting watering usually allow you to water food plants as necessary. For a garden divided into several beds, it might be worthwhile to install a separate shutoff valve at the head of each one. Then you can open and close sections as their watering needs change—when one bed has sprouting vegetables yet others lie fallow, for example.

Vegetable gardens need frequent cultivation, which can damage irrigation lines. To get around this, use PVC pipe buried 18 inches deep as the supply line. Bring it aboveground with an elbow in a secure spot, and stake heavily so it is solid. Then set up the header and lateral lines using a quick-clip hose-fitting system, the kind used for changing rapidly from one hand sprinkler to another. This will require several adapters, but the result is a system that can be pulled out quickly whenever cultivation is required. In cold climates, bring aboveground sections indoors for the winter.

IRRIGATING VEGETABLE BEDS

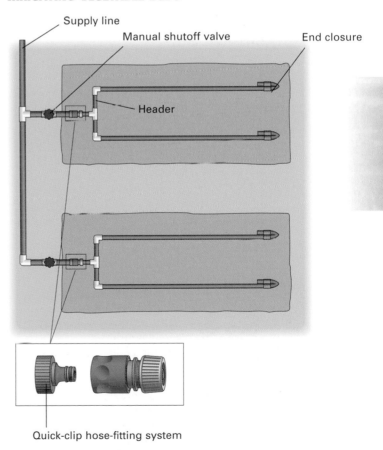

Supply line

Manual shutoff valve

End closure

Header

Quick-clip hose-fitting system

An automatic controller allows you to set different watering times and durations for a number of circuits. This weatherproof unit is wired into the home's electrical system through the junction box and conduit on the right. The conduit on the left conceals multiple-stranded, low-voltage wire that runs below ground to automatic sprinkler valves.

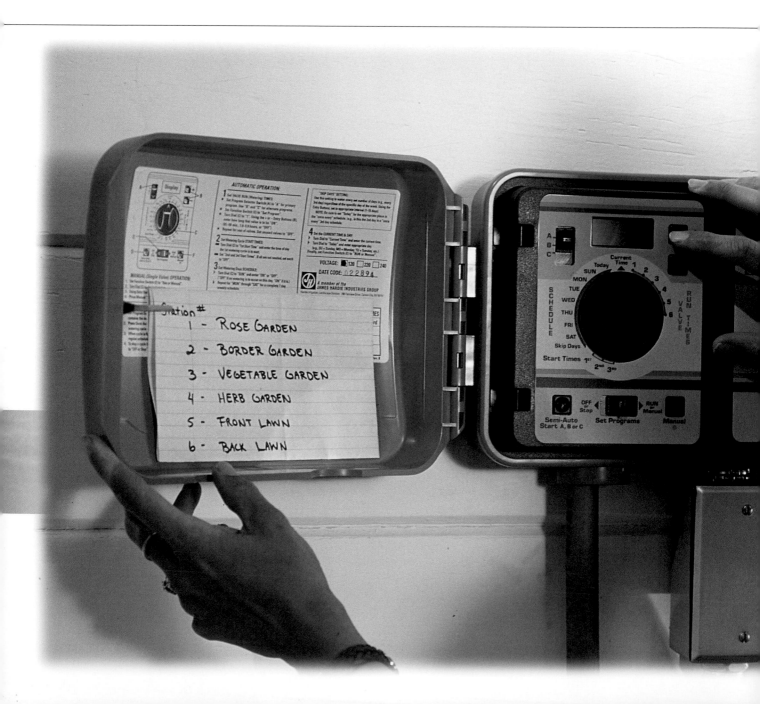

USING AND REPAIRING AN IRRIGATION SYSTEM

Once you have chosen the irrigation system you want, it's time to decide how you want to operate, maintain, and repair it. Will you control it manually, automatically, or a combination of both? Next, determine how much water to apply and when. This is not overly complicated, but will require some time for figuring, testing, and adjusting. The irrigation system will need routine maintenance to function at its best. You may find, too, that watering needs change over time. When this happens, consider modifying the system to accommodate the change. Even in the best planned system, things can go wrong. If they do, consult Problem Solving, page 93.

USING YOUR SYSTEM

The best time to irrigate is early in the morning, when still air and cool temperatures reduce evaporation, and warmth from the sun will dry off the plants.

Now that your irrigation system is installed and operational, you still need to resolve a few questions. Just how automated do you want your system to be? How much, and on what kind of schedule, should you water? It will be easier to make these decisions if you first understand the basic principles of watering.

HOW MUCH TO WATER

Overwatering wastes water and can lead to disease or rot; underwatering stunts plant growth and can kill sensitive plants. The zone between those two extremes is, fortunately, broad. Most plants will grow and thrive when the ground varies between very moist and somewhat dry.

Old theories advocated watering to the point of saturation, then not watering again until the soil was dry. With drip systems, especially, gardeners used to place emitters in small numbers near the base of a plant (instead of evenly throughout the garden as is now recommended) and run the system for hours in order to water deeply, then allow the plant to dry out almost to the point of wilting before watering it again. The result was irregular growth and considerable water loss, because much of the water went, not to the plant, but to rehydrate the parched soil. Of course, infrequent but deep waterings are better than frequent, excessively shallow ones. The ideal situation, however, is to keep the soil moist at all times, both near the surface and to a depth of at least 2 to 3 feet. This shallow upper layer of soil is where most of the root hairs, through which plants absorb water, minerals, and oxygen, are found. There is no particular need to water to great depths; deeper-growing roots (sinker roots) serve mainly to anchor plants.

WHEN TO WATER

To irrigate properly, each of the circuits in the yard must be on its own schedule. One of the reasons you divided the system into circuits was to meet the individual needs of plantings. Only one circuit can be operated at a given time without overloading the system. Circuits can be run alternately, one coming on as another closes down, or on separate days, or even several times a day—depending on each circuit's needs.

The ideal time of day for sprinkler irrigation is just before dawn. There is usually little wind to divert spray, and water pressure is at its maximum. Because there is no burning sun to cause water to evaporate, more water enters the soil, and therefore, the plants' cells, than during the heat of the day. The next best time to irrigate is in the evening. This is often the time people choose to run manual irrigation systems, since few people want to get up at 3 a.m. to turn on the sprinkler. Evening irrigation, however, has two disadvantages. First, water pressure is usually slightly lower. Second, diseases are more likely to infect susceptible plants when leaves remain moist through the night. With early morning watering, the leaves soon dry off under the heat of the sun.

The least efficient time of day to water is at midday. On a hot, dry day, especially if there is a bit of wind, most of the water sprayed evaporates before it ever enters the soil.

Since most micro-irrigation systems, especially those emitting water underground or under a cover of mulch, do not produce a spray, there is less danger of water loss due to evaporation or of spreading disease. You can, therefore, run your micro-irrigation system at any time.

MANUAL SYSTEMS

These are the most basic systems. You control the irrigation entirely, turning it on and off as needed. The main advantage of manual irrigation is it keeps you in close contact with the yard and its needs. This contrasts strongly with an automatic system, with which you can easily forget that human intervention occasionally might be useful. No automatic system yet created, for example, will turn off a sprinkler system on a windy day when much of the water will be blown onto the street. If you have a manual system, you will probably notice such water loss. You will probably also be aware that irrigation needs are less during cold weather. If you depend on an automatic system, you might not observe such changes.

A knowledgeable gardener can keep a watchful eye on all plantings

and turn the water on and off as needed. Often a finger sunk into the earth daily will give all the information you need. If the soil feels dry to the touch, it requires watering; if it feels wet, it shouldn't be irrigated.

Manual systems are most practical when the yard is small or when only parts of it—such as a vegetable garden—are irrigated. As the irrigated area increases in size and variety, running your system manually is more complicated.

Another major drawback to manual irrigation is your availability, or lack of it. To run such a system efficiently, you have to be available throughout the entire growing season and—given the watering restrictions in many towns and cities—often at odd hours of the day or night. No wonder city dwellers in particular are keen on automated systems.

MANUAL-ON, AUTOMATIC-OFF

This is the most basic derivative of manual irrigation. You decide when to turn on the circuit, but a simple controller turns it off. This is enormously practical if you want a manual system but are required by municipal regulations to run the system at night. You can turn it on before you go to bed and be assured that it will turn off the water again as

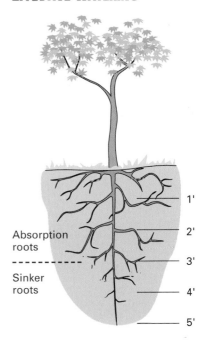

Absorption roots

Sinker roots

1'
2'
3'
4'
5'

A manual-on, automatic-off valve uses a timer so it shuts off after a pre-set interval. This allows you to switch the system on at any time, safe in the knowledge that it will shut itself off.

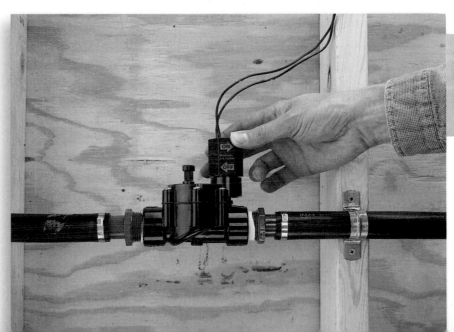

USING YOUR SYSTEM

continued

A battery-controlled timer turns off water to one circuit.

Two multistation controllers (left) and a stand-alone controller (right).

you sleep. It's also handy if you are the least bit forgetful. Many homeowners turn on the system, but then get busy with another task and forget to turn it off. This not only wastes water but could cause serious erosion problems and damage to plants and garden infrastructures. Manual micro-irrigation systems are particularly easy to forget, because there is often no outward sign that the system is running—until the basement begins filling with water.

Most automatic-off controllers are simple, inexpensive, and require no electrical hookup or batteries. Connect the controller to the system at any point after the control valve. Just twist the dial to set the length of time or the number of gallons.

AUTOMATIC WATERING

For people who travel a great deal or simply prefer the convenience of a system that runs itself, fully automatic controllers are a necessity. They take most of the effort out of watering and don't make demands on your time. And they don't have to cost much.

There is little point in discussing specific controller types, because each company's products have different characteristics. Additionally, the field is evolving so quickly that any models mentioned here might be out-of-date. It will be more useful for you to review the following information about the different functions offered. Then, once you have an idea of your needs, you can shop around. Consult the manufacturer's instructions for specific installation and operating information on your model.

STAND-ALONE CONTROLLERS: These battery-operated controllers are designed to be connected to individual circuits and are usually attached to the manifold immediately after the vacuum breaker. Most have digital or liquid-crystal display clocks that must first be set for the current time, the days that watering is required, and the time and duration of irrigation. If your circuit requires more than one watering period in the same day (which could be the case with slopes or container plantings, for instance), make sure the stand-alone controller you choose allows several start times per day.

Stand-alone controllers are most useful with a limited number of circuits—usually no more than three. If you have several circuits you will find it less expensive to install a multistation controller than to add one to each circuit. Also, a good deal of mental gymnastics is required to integrate the watering times of a series of stand-alone controllers without two circuits overlapping.

MULTISTATION CONTROLLERS: As prices on multistation controllers become more reasonable, these units—once strictly the domain of the wealthy—are rapidly becoming the norm in home irrigation systems. From a single location, you can control all the circuits in both front and backyards. Their operation is simple: Wires lead from the

ADDITIONAL CONTROLLER OPTIONS

Multistation controllers offer many options. Each additional option generally increases the price of the controller, so you need to decide which are most vital to the correct organization of your irrigation system.

Make sure the model you choose is easy to program. Some are simple; others may seem as complicated as programming a computer from scratch. Have an irrigation dealer demonstrate a few models, then go back later and try to program them on your own.

A local dealer can be of enormous help in suggesting exactly which functions are most appropriate for your needs. Here are some of your choices.

■ **STATION TIMING.** Most controllers have both a minimum and a maximum run time. If you use emitters, where the circuit often needs to run for several hours at a time, make sure you purchase a controller with station timing at least as along as the longest anticipated run time for your circuit. At the other extreme, if you intend to use misters, remember they may need only a minute or so of irrigation at a time, so look for a controller offering short run times.

■ **START TIMES PER DAY.** Some controllers offer only one start time per circuit per day. This may be sufficient for many micro-irrigation uses, but not enough for sprinkler systems, especially those on slopes or clay soils that may need several short periods of watering during the same day. Other controllers have 10 or more start times per day, which is probably excessive for most needs, but will be useful if you intend to use misters.

■ **WATERING SCHEDULE.** There are dozens of possibilities: 7-day weeks, odd-even day intervals, 1- to 30-day intervals, etcetera. Seven-day schedules are sufficient when dealing with municipal watering regulations, as they usually allow three watering days out of seven. Odd-even day intervals, for watering every second day, usually suffice where such regulations don't exist. For situations in which a great deal of flexibility is required, such as systems with several very different circuits, you can find controllers that allow an almost infinite combination of schedules. Those with 365-day calendars make it possible to program the entire season in advance, including increased watering in dry months.

■ **BATTERY BACKUP.** This feature makes sure your programming isn't erased during a power failure. Controllers with 365-day calendars allow you to disconnect the timer for the winter and plug it back in during the spring; it has the program, current time, and date stored in memory and will be ready for action.

■ **RAIN-OFF FEATURE.** Most controllers include a rain-off feature of some sort, which allows you to cancel watering when it rains. Some even allow you to program several days without irrigation, ideal when enough rain falls in one day to keep all plantings watered for a week.

■ **MANUAL OVERRIDE.** This feature allows you to water outside the normally programmed hours. It is useful for spot watering and for spray adjustments and other verifications.

■ **MASTER VALVE CIRCUIT.** This circuit helps prevent water loss should something go wrong. A separate automatic valve will be needed as a master valve. This same circuit can also be used to activate a remote pump if the system requires one.

■ **SENSOR FUNCTIONS.** These features allow the controller to override the programmed irrigation schedule when an attached sensor (see Water Sensors, page 82) indicates no water is needed.

controller to automatic control valves at the start of each circuit, and the controller sends an electric signal to the control valves telling them when to turn on and off.

Each controller has stations for a specific number of irrigation circuits. Make sure the controller you choose has enough stations to cover all the circuits you've planned. You may want to have one extra unused station in case your watering needs change and you must add a circuit.

Multistation controllers vary in appearance and means of operation. Some are fully electronic, with digital or liquid-crystal-display devices with adjustable bars or buttons; some are electromechanical, operating with dials and little pins, much like the timers used to turn lights on and off automatically indoors; and others are a combination of the two. You can also run the system from a home computer. Soon, it may even be possible to hook up, via computer, to weather stations in order to set up your irrigation schedule according to the specifics of local weather. How the various multistation controllers work, however, is less important than whether the controller is capable of meeting your watering needs.

With multistation controllers, you begin by entering the time, then the date and day of the week, followed by the watering program for each circuits in your yard. How you do so depends on the type of controller. The most basic controllers have only one program, that is, choice of days in the week in which the irrigation turns on and off. In this case, you can operate each circuit at a different time, but only on the days you have programmed. Other controllers have two or more programs. With a two-program model, you could, for example, set certain circuits to come on three times a week, and others only once a week—and on a different day, at that. In all cases, be sure only one circuit be in operation at one time. With most multistation controllers, this is automatically ensured within each program

USING YOUR SYSTEM
continued

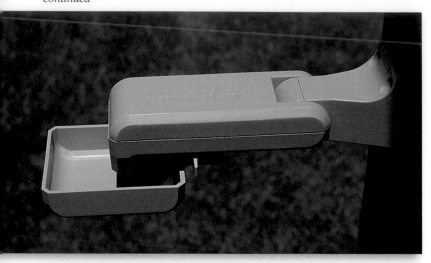

An automatic rain shutoff (top) or moisture sensors (bottom) make an automatic controller even more efficient.

several. The danger of controlling several sectors with one sensor, however, is that irrigation needs usually vary; if your lot is irregular, a single sensor per circuit is often better. Also, even within a circuit, there are areas that dry out more quickly or remain moist longer than others. You may have to experiment to find which sensor placement gives the most accurate general reading for the entire circuit.

■ AUTOMATIC RAIN SHUTOFFS: These measure rainfall rather than soil moisture. Although this may seem like a flaw, the devices are the better choice in many climates because you can assume all parts of the yard receive about the same rainfall. Therefore, a well-placed single rain-shutoff device can suffice for the entire yard. The unit operates by catching a small amount of rainwater. Electrodes then measure the water level, and when there is more than a given depth (this can be adjusted), they cut off the controller. It resumes its normal functions when the water level drops. An automatic rain shutoff should be placed in a spot that represents normal conditions for the sector it controls: neither too shady nor too sunny, yet fully exposed to rainfall.

Rain-shutoff and moisture-sensor devices make irrigation easier, but they are not a panacea. You still may need to override the system manually under special circumstances and may often have to adjust the devices slightly to mesh with your needs. Ask a local irrigation dealer which devices are best for your climate and condition. Some may be more reliable than others under your particular circumstances.

AUTOMATIC CONTROL VALVES: A multistation controller is useless unless it is connected to automatic control valves. Also called remote-control valves, these include various kinds—in-line valves and antisiphon valves. They are designed to shut water on or off following an appropriate electronic impulse. The same type of automatic control valve can be used as both a master valve and a circuit control valve (see Control Valve Hookup, page 55).

If your system is new, put in automatic control valves as you install the piping, then use multiple-stranded wire to connect each valve to the multistation controller. Put in at least one strand more than the number of circuits to use as a common wire and, if possible, one or two others for future circuits. For line runs less than 800 feet long, use 18-gauge irrigation wire (sometimes referred to as plastic-jacketed thermostat wire). For longer runs, use 14-gauge wire. The wire can be run along the trenches already dug for the piping, although it may be necessary to dig a short,

by the controller's means of operation: each station is turned on as the previous one goes off. However, when two or more programs are available, the controller may not prevent one from infringing on the other's run time. It's up to you to make sure this doesn't happen.

WATER SENSORS: These popular devices fill in one of the last gaps in automatic watering: making sure that the system doesn't come on when water is not needed. Moisture sensors and automatic rain-shutoff devices both override the controller to prevent irrigation; the only difference is how they do so. They are especially useful in climates where summer rainfall is frequent but variable.

■ MOISTURE SENSORS: These are inserted in the soil, where they measure the amount of moisture present. Many can be adjusted to different moisture levels, depending on the needs of the plants in the sector. They can usually be used to control one circuit or

WIRING FOR A CONTROLLER

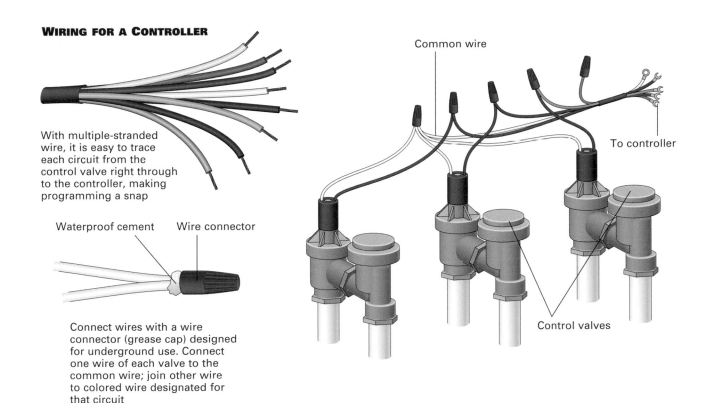

With multiple-stranded wire, it is easy to trace each circuit from the control valve right through to the controller, making programming a snap

Waterproof cement   Wire connector

Connect wires with a wire connector (grease cap) designed for underground use. Connect one wire of each valve to the common wire; join other wire to colored wire designated for that circuit

Common wire

To controller

Control valves

separate trench to lead the wires to the location of the controller. If possible, lay the wire under the pipe and make sure it is not touching any rocks or other abrasive material that might cut into the insulation. Wire should not be in contact with metal pipe as this increases the danger of current leakage and short circuits. If any wire will be in a trench by itself, especially in a garden area where digging might occur, run it through a length of PVC pipe to protect it from shovel damage.

It is easy to convert manual antisiphon valves to an automatic system. Turn off the water to the valves, remove the manual valve stem (but not the complete valve body) with a crescent wrench, and replace it with an appropriate automatic valve adapter. An irrigation dealer can help you select one suitable for your valve type. Then connect the adapters to the controller, shown at bottom right.

CONNECTING THE CONTROLLER: Locate a multistation controller in a dry spot that is readily accessible and near a power source. Many multistation controllers are for indoor use only and are generally installed in the basement or garage. Others are built into weatherproof boxes and can be used indoors or out. It is sometimes cheaper to buy two smaller multistation controllers (four-, six-, and eight-station controllers are standard) than one larger one; if so, you might like to

locate the controllers near the manifolds—one in the front and one in the back. If you have more than one controller, be careful to set them so only one circuit is in use at any one time.

HOOKING UP TO THE CONTROLLER

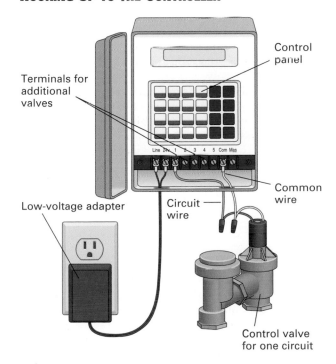

Control panel

Terminals for additional valves

Common wire

Low-voltage adapter

Circuit wire

Control valve for one circuit

USING YOUR SYSTEM
continued

Before connecting the wires leading from the automatic control valves to the controller, make sure the power is shut off to the controller. There will be two wires leading from each automatic valve. One is the circuit wire, and it should be run to a numbered terminal screw on the controller. The other is the common, or ground, wire. In multiple-stranded wire, each wire has a different-colored plastic coating; choose a different color for the hot wire of each valve and one other color as the common wire. Attach each hot wire to a station in the controller box and note which wire color and station corresponds to which circuit. Connect the common wires of the various valves and run only the one common wire to the common wire terminal screw of the controller. You can now plug in the controller and begin to program it.

CREATING AN IRRIGATION SCHEDULE

The purpose of irrigation is to get the right amount of water to all the plants at the right time. To do so, you'll have to analyze the yard's needs, prepare a watering schedule, and adjust the schedule as needed.

SPRINKLER IRRIGATION: Your goal as a home irrigator is to replace the water lost by evaporation and transpiration, as well as to supply the very small amount that actually goes into plant growth. For that reason, it is useful to know the local evapotranspiration rate: the water typically lost during a given month. You can obtain this from a local irrigation dealer, a Cooperative Extension agent, or the weather bureau. You might find, for example, that the evapotranspiration rate is 7 or 8 inches per month in July, but only one-third that in November. For ideal plant growth, you have to try to replace water lost through evapotranspiration and not compensated for by rainfall. As a simple mathematical equation, irrigation equals evapotranspiration minus precipitation.

Many homeowners use instinct to work out an irrigation program. They simply turn the system on when they judge the plants need water, and off when the soil seems saturated. There's nothing wrong with doing so, but generally, plant growth will be uneven because this kind of care can't help but be slightly irregular. Also, if you automate the watering system, you will need to base your settings on something more than instinct.

You can also approximate watering needs and use them to develop a watering schedule. For example, most lawn areas need about ½ inch of rain every second day. Most spray heads could deliver ½ inch of precipitation in about 30 minutes; a rotary head would take three times as long, or 90 minutes, to deliver that amount of water. Up to twice that amount of irrigation would be needed in hot, dry weather and only about half that amount in cool weather. You could use these

INFILTRATION RATE FOR LEVEL GROUND AND SLOPES

Average infiltration rate in inches/hour

Soil Texture Type	Percent of Slope				
	0–4.9%	5–7.9%	8–11.9%	12–15.9%	Over 16%
Coarse Sand	1.25	1.00	0.75	0.50	0.31
Medium Sand	1.06	0.85	0.64	0.42	0.27
Fine Sand	0.94	0.75	0.56	0.38	0.24
Loamy Sand	0.88	0.70	0.53	0.35	0.22
Sandy Loam	0.75	0.60	0.45	0.30	0.19
Fine Sandy Loam	0.63	0.50	0.38	0.25	0.16
Very Fine Sandy Loam	0.59	0.47	0.35	0.24	0.15
Loam	0.54	0.43	0.33	0.22	0.14
Silt Loam	0.50	0.40	0.30	0.20	0.13
Silt	0.44	0.35	0.26	0.18	0.11
Sandy Clay	0.31	0.25	0.19	0.12	0.08
Clay Loam	0.25	0.20	0.15	0.10	0.06
Silty Clay	0.19	0.15	0.11	0.08	0.05
Clay	0.13	0.10	0.08	0.05	0.03

PREPARING YOUR OWN IRRIGATION CHART

It is easiest to have a local irrigation supplier work out a watering schedule for you, but if you want to do it on your own, here are the basics.

1. Find out the precipitation rate for each of your circuits by using the chart supplied by the manufacturer for each type of head or emitter. For sprinkler systems, two rates are usually given: one for square spacing and the other for triangular spacing. Choose the appropriate rate for each circuit.

2. Determine the evapotranspiration rate per week for each month of the growing season for the region. You can get the rate per month from a county extension agent or the weather bureau. Divide this amount by four to get the rate per week.

3. Determine the infiltration rate for each circuit using the chart on page 84.

4. Prepare a separate irrigation chart for each month based on the information above.

Irrigation Chart

	Precipitation Rate (Precip. Rate) *(inches/hour)*	Evapo-transpiration Rate (ET Rate) *(inches/week)*	Infiltration Rate (IF Rate) *(inches/hour)*	Total Weekly Irrigation Time *(minutes/week)*	Minutes Without Runoff	Number of Cycles Needed*	Number of Minutes per Cycle
	(According to manufacturer)	(Monthly ET Rate ÷ 4)	(See chart, on page 84)	(ET Rate × 60 minutes ÷ Precip. Rate)	(IF Rate × 60 minutes ÷ Precip. Rate)	(Total Weekly Irrigation Time ÷ Minutes Without Runoff)	(Total Weekly Irrigation Time ÷ Number of Cycles Needed)
Circuit 1							
Circuit 2							
Circuit 3							
Circuit 4							
Circuit 5							
Circuit 6							
Circuit 7							
Circuit 8							

*Always round up this figure to the next highest number. For example, 4.1 would be 5.

Let's assume you have the following information:

1. The irrigation supplier gives you the precipitation rates for three circuits: 0.5 inch per hour for circuit 1; 0.8 inch per hour for circuit 2; and 0.35 inch per hour for circuit 3.

2. The evapotranspiration rate for the month is 5.4 inches. Divided by four, this gives you a weekly rate of 1.35.

3. Your soil is a clay loam throughout the three circuits and there is no appreciable slope, giving you an infiltration rate of 0.25 inch per hour (see chart on page 84).

Fill in the irrigation chart with the information you gathered, then perform the calculations to fill in the rest of the chart.

You can now determine a watering schedule by adding the number of cycles needed per circuit and the number of minutes of irrigation for each circuit.

Irrigation Chart Sample

	Precipitation Rate *(inches/hour)*	Evapo-transpiration Rate (ET Rate) *(inches/week)*	Infiltration Rate (IF Rate) *(inches/hour)*	Total Weekly Irrigation Time *(minutes/week)*	Minutes Without Runoff	Number of Cycles Needed*	Number of Minutes per Cycle
Circuit 1	0.5	1.35	0.25	162	30	6 (5.4 rounded up)	27
Circuit 2	0.8	1.35	0.25	101	19	6 (5.3 rounded up)	17
Circuit 3	0.35	1.35	0.25	231.43	45	6 (5.1 rounded up)	39

USING YOUR SYSTEM
continued

WATERING GUIDELINES FOR MICRO-IRRIGATION SYSTEMS

Weather	Duration in Hours	Number of Times Per Week
Cool	2	1 or 2
Warm	3	2
Hot	4	3

approximations to set up a fairly workable watering schedule.

You may have to factor in more than one irrigation session per day, because clay soils or slopes can't absorb ½ inch of rain in only 30 minutes (the output of an average spray head). Instead you might want to apply ¼ inch either for 15 minutes on two different days or in two separate sessions of 15 minutes in one day (leave at least 60 minutes between the two consecutive irrigations). This calculation is a basic one because it considers only a few of the possible factors, so be prepared to adjust the irrigation program if you find some circuits are not getting enough water and others are receiving too much.

There is an easier way to come up with a precise watering schedule for each circuit: ask the irrigation supplier who drew up your plan to calculate it for you. The supplier should be able to estimate of the number of times each circuit on the system should be run per week and for how long, taking into account soil and irrigation type and the rate of precipitation of each circuit.

If you can't get this information, calculate the number of cycles and the number of minutes to run each cycle (see page 85).

MICRO-IRRIGATION: Because water is applied slowly with micro-irrigation, there is essentially no danger of runoff, not even on slopes or clay soils. This is important, because micro-irrigation usually runs for long periods. Most people find they can irrigate efficiently without doing any complicated calculations. Just ask an irrigation supplier what kind of irrigation program is recommended, or use the guidelines in the chart at left.

You may need to increase the number of hours per irrigation cycle for trees and larger shrubs and decrease them for arid-climate plants, as well as make adjustments according to soil type. For information on timing the watering of container plants (see "Container Gardens: A Special Case," page 74).

DRAWING UP A SCHEDULE: Once you know how many irrigation cycles you'll need for each circuit and how long each should last, decide when to run each cycle. There are two important factors here: Each cycle must be run separately from all others, and if you intend to provide two or more cycles for the same circuit on a given day, you must leave at least an hour between cycles. This allows the water from the first cycle to be absorbed by the time the second begins.

You can water daily, every second day, three times a week, or whatever is appropriate, as long as each circuit gets its required precipitation during that period. However, it is better to water each circuit deeply a few times a week than lightly every day. Many people prefer to limit their irrigation cycles to two or three days a week.

To visualize the watering schedule before posting it on a wall for manual irrigation or programming it into the automatic controller, draw up a chart. It should include the days of the week and the times when each circuit should be turned on and off. If local watering restrictions apply, you must irrigate only on the days and at the times permitted.

See the sample watering schedule on page 87, which is for a municipality that limits watering to Mondays, Wednesdays, and Thursdays between midnight and 6 a.m. The data used were taken from "Preparing Your Own Irrigation Chart," page 85.

In this example, water restrictions apply; the first step is to compare the hours when watering is permitted with the total number of hours of irrigation required by the circuits (this is calculated by adding up the figures in the chart "Total Weekly Irrigation Time" on page 85). It becomes clear in the sample schedule that it won't be necessary to water on all three permitted days, as only about 8½

"FERTIGATION"

Fertilizing as you irrigate, or "fertigation," is not feasible for high-pressure sprinkler systems. Most of the fertilizer would be wasted and could pose a health hazard. With a micro-irrigation system, however, you may be able to use a device like the one shown here. Check with a local irrigation dealer to see if fertigation would work with your system.

FERTILIZING AUTOMATICALLY

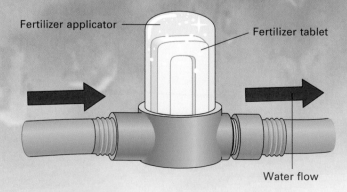

Fertilizer applicator

Fertilizer tablet

Water flow

SAMPLE WATERING SCHEDULE

	Sunday	Monday	Tuesday	Wednesday	Thursday	Friday	Saturday
First Cycle							
Circuit 1		12:00–12:27			12:00–12:27		
Circuit 2		12:28–12:45			12:28–12:45		
Circuit 3		12:46–1:25			12:46–1:25		
Second Cycle*							
Circuit 1		1:27–1:54			1:27–1:54		
Circuit 2		1:55–2:12			1:55–2:12		
Circuit 3		2:25–3:04			2:25–3:04		
Third Cycle*							
Circuit 1		2:54–3:21			2:54–3:21		
Circuit 2		3:22–3:39			3:22–3:39		
Circuit 3		4:04–4:43			4:04–4:43		

* Note that the second and third cycles don't start until one hour after the previous cycle is completed. An automatic system will not repeat irrigation on the same circuit until one hour has elapsed to allow time for the water to soak into the soil. For example, the first cycle of circuit 1 ends at 12:27 pm, and the second cycle doesn't begin until 1:27 p.m.

hours of irrigation are needed, yet 18 are available. Because deep waterings are preferable to frequent shallow ones, the irrigations are concentrated in only two days. The six cycles required for each circuit can, therefore, be divided into three cycles for each watering day.

MAKING ADJUSTMENTS: After using a new irrigation program for a few weeks, you'll probably need to make adjustments. Some circuits may need longer or more frequent irrigation sessions than originally planned, and others less. Adjust the programming until plants are getting enough water with no puddles or excess runoff.

You will also need to adjust according to weather conditions. During unseasonably warm periods, manually override an automatic system and add a watering period. Under cooler-than-average conditions, you might skip a watering. Any precipitation will also affect watering needs. If you don't use a sensor, you may want to use a rain gauge to check how many inches fell, then subtract that amount from the month's evapotranspiration rate to see how many irrigation cycles to skip. Plants that are growing extremely rapidly may need longer or more frequent irrigations.

A few simple calculations will help you take the guesswork out of scheduling sprinklers.

PERFORMING ROUTINE MAINTENANCE

Properly designed irrigation systems require only minimal maintenance. However, a little upkeep is vital. And as time passes, you may find that you want to adapt your system to changing needs.

CHECKING SYSTEM OPERATION

At installation time and at the beginning of each season, check the system thoroughly. Turn on each circuit individually and make sure the water is reaching all areas it is supposed to cover. Most adjustments are easy to make. During the season, simply keep an eye open for problems. Some of the signs that the system needs minor adjustments are spray reaching unwanted parts of the yard, areas that remain dry after spraying, and excessive puddling or runoff.

Visual checks are easiest to make with sprinkler systems, because it is simple to see how they are spraying and if the water is reaching the intended areas. Micro-irrigation needs more careful attention. You may have to get down on your knees and push aside a bit of mulch to be sure that water is indeed dripping from each nozzle. Subsurface emitter lines and porous pipe systems are more difficult to verify, because the soil can be completely dry on the surface yet moist underneath. Puddles of water on the surface can indicate leaks, overly long watering periods, or pressure problems. Sectors where plant growth is stunted or withered while nearby areas are green and growing could indicate a plugged emitter or a pinched pipe. Finally, check any humidity sensors annually.

CLEANING AND FLUSHING

All irrigation systems need to be cleaned occasionally to remove dirt, debris, or plant materials that have built up over the seasons. Take some time now to review these procedures to ensure that water can run freely through your irrigation system.

SPRINKLER SYSTEMS: Dirt and debris can accumulate in the pipes, risers, and nozzles of a system. To prevent buildup, flush out the system at least once a year. With the system turned off, remove individual nozzles and heads, then turn on the water for a few minutes until a clean, solid stream flows from each head. Turn off the water. Take apart the nozzles (depending on the type, this can be done by hand or with a screwdriver, or a special key may be needed) and clean them to remove any dirt. Rinse out the screen or filter basket as well. Reassemble and replace all the parts. Turn on the circuit again to check that everything is operating properly.

Make sure you keep the lawn mown around stationary and pop-up lawn heads so grass won't block the spray. You may occasionally need to prune vegetation growing around spray heads in garden, ground cover, and shrub areas.

MICRO-IRRIGATION SYSTEMS: Micro-irrigation systems are more sensitive to blocking by dirt and debris than spray systems are, so they should be cleaned more

The supply line for a new valve should be flushed out before the valve is installed.

frequently. Once a month during the operating season, remove the end closure from each line and flush the line thoroughly until the water runs clear, then put the end closure back in place.

Flush the filter monthly. Most can be flushed simply by turning on the flush outlet (dump valve). Otherwise, take out the filter and rinse it. Even filters that have a flush outlet should be taken apart, cleaned, and inspected at least once a year. If the screen inside shows any sign of damage, replace it.

ADJUSTING FOR COVERAGE AND SPRAY

At installation and at the beginning of each season, as well as during the season if there is an obvious problem, check for proper coverage from each spray head. The heads may have been knocked out of alignment by a careless foot, a wayward lawn mower, or a snow shovel. This can cause them to spray sidewalks or other unintended surfaces while leaving part of the garden unwatered. There might also be too much or not enough overlap between heads. To make adjustments, either remove the nozzle to redirect its spray, turn the flow adjustment screw on the top of the nozzle, or use a special ratchet. Most rotary heads have a friction collar at their base that can be used to adjust the angle, and a diffuser screw to adjust the distance of throw. With micro-sprinklers, you can simply twist the head to change its direction.

Sometimes spray heads produce a mist or fogging action rather that the large drops necessary. This indicates the water flow is too strong. It can be adjusted simply at the circuit control valve. If the system is manual, turn the system shutoff clockwise until you see large drops. Automatic valves have a special knob for this adjustment.

WINTERIZING

Although some manufacturers claim their systems can withstand freezing conditions if automatic drains are installed at the lowest point in each circuit, thoroughly draining the system each winter is always worthwhile in freezing climates. To do so, drain all water from the circuit by turning off the main valve and

running each circuit for a few minutes. Next blow any remaining water from the control valves using an air compressor (compressors can usually be rented). Repeat for each circuit until the entire system is clear of water. It's best to bring any aboveground sections of a micro-irrigation system indoors for the winter. In spring, when the ground has completely thawed, reinstall any micro-irrigation piping removed the previous fall, turn the main valve back on, and check out the system carefully (see page 88).

Disconnect stand-alone controllers and bring them in for the winter. Unplug multistation controllers remove the battery unless the battery keeps the controller programmed for the entire winter. Replace the battery with a new one each spring.

ADAPTING TO CHANGING NEEDS

Your garden will probably change, and so will its watering demands. Often you may need only to readjust the watering schedule or adjust the flow of sprinklers, but if you've added new beds or radically altered the use of any part of the yard, you must make more significant changes.

For many sprinkler heads, a screwdriver is the only tool you need to make adjustments.

Use an air compressor to clear sprinkler lines before the winter freeze.

PERFORMING ROUTINE MAINTENANCE
continued

ADDING TO AN ESTABLISHED SYSTEM

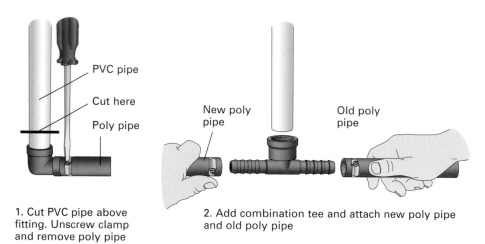

PVC pipe

Cut here

Poly pipe

1. Cut PVC pipe above fitting. Unscrew clamp and remove poly pipe

New poly pipe

Old poly pipe

2. Add combination tee and attach new poly pipe and old poly pipe

Modifications to aboveground micro-irrigation systems are easy to carry out, especially if you left room on each circuit for future additions. Just add line and punch in new emitters (see "Surface Installation," page 68). You can also replace emitters and micro-sprinklers with some of higher or lower output (or, in the case of micro-sprinklers, of a different pattern). Just be sure to recalculate the circuit's capacity before adding any component to avoid overloading it. To

ADDING A NEW PVC LINE

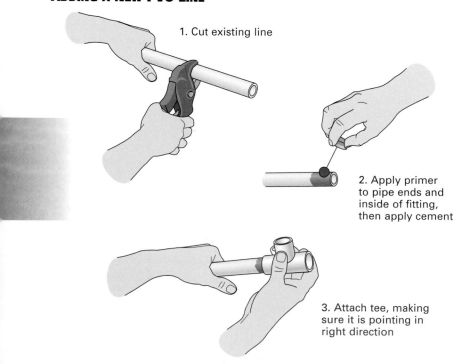

1. Cut existing line

2. Apply primer to pipe ends and inside of fitting, then apply cement

3. Attach tee, making sure it is pointing in right direction

remove any lines or emitters, simply install hole plugs (see "Repairing Blunders," page 72). Subsurface micro-irrigation installations require digging, of course, but the process is otherwise similar (see "Subsurface Supply-Line Installation," page 70).

Adding modifications to sprinkler systems is not complicated if you left space on each circuit for future development, but some digging will generally be necessary. Before adding an extra sprinkler head or pipe to a circuit, check that enough pressure is available on the circuit. Dig carefully so you don't break the pipe or other fixtures already in place; then dig whatever trenches are necessary for the new section.

See pages 51–57 to learn how to install new pipe and fixtures. Any PVC fittings that are cut out as you make changes will have to be replaced, because you won't be able to remove the solvent that cements them to the pipe. Polyethylene fittings, however, can usually be reused. Spray heads and risers can also be used again.

Sometimes modifying a sprinkler system is as simple as changing a few sprinkler heads or even just the nozzles. With many modern sprinkler heads, for example, a full-circle nozzle can be replaced with a part circle or even a strip nozzle in a matter of seconds. When lawn sections are converted into shrub or flower beds, sometimes the change is as simple as placing the lawn sprinkler heads on higher risers. Be certain, though, that any sprinklers that will be added or changed will be compatible with others on the circuit. You couldn't convert, for example, only two rotary heads on a circuit to spray heads.

Any major changes could require the addition of a new circuit. Once again, the process is much easier if you left space in the original system—for example, a manifold closed with a cap rather than an elbow, or a controller with at least one extra station.

REPAIRING THE SYSTEM

Fortunately, little can go wrong with a properly installed irrigation system Malfunctions are the exception rather than the rule. If something does go wrong, here's how to diagnose the problem.

TROUBLESHOOTING YOUR SYSTEM

To discover the cause of irrigation system malfunctions, consult "Problem Solving," page 93. Most potential problems can be noted and corrected during routine maintenance. Regular flushing and cleaning, especially of filters and sprinkler heads, will eliminate most problems before any serious damage is done. Some problems may need more vigorous intervention.

LOCATING LEAKS: Leaks are the most pernicious of irrigation problems. They can go unnoticed for long periods, and often the only symptom of a minor leak is that the system operates less and less efficiently over time. Only when the problem becomes more serious does water buildup saturate the ground, a sign there is a leak in the sector.

If you suspect a leak in an aboveground section of the circuit (this is likely only with micro-irrigation), the source of the problem is easy enough to trace. Remove any mulch, turn on the circuit, and check for any unwanted bubbling or spraying.

Leaky sections of underground pipe are much harder to locate. When a leak is suspected in a high-pressure irrigation system, cap off all the spray heads, turn on the circuit, and wait until the appearance of surface water indicates where the leak is located. If you can't find the leak call in a professional, who can use special equipment to trace it. Otherwise, you will have to dig, and without knowing where to begin, you may unearth much of the system before finding the leak.

REPAIRING PIPE DAMAGE: Improper seals of poly-pipe joints can be corrected simply by tightening the clamps where the leak occurs. Small leaks in poly or PVC pipe can be repaired easily with a hole plug or with a repair coupling, also called a dresser coupling. To install a repair coupling, turn off the water and use plastic-pipe shears or a hacksaw to cut through the pipe at the leak. Then move the two pipe ends far enough apart to slip on the repair coupling components, center the coupling body over the cut, and tighten the coupling nuts and gaskets until firmly in place.

Major leaks in poly, PVC, or any other kind of pipe mean that the damaged section must be replaced. It is best to insert an additional length of pipe wherever connections have been pulled apart, because this kind of damage, often the result of deep frost causing the line to contract, is likely to recur. Leaks in PVC pipes, unlike those in poly pipe, can be repaired only by replacing the damaged section. Repairing pipe is as simple as cutting out the damaged section and inserting new pipe and joints (see page 51).

Always turn off the water before making repairs; then check the system and flush it thoroughly before reburying the pipe. Poly-pipe fittings near damaged sections can be reused if they are still in good condition, but don't attempt to repair fittings near damaged PVC pipe: just cut them out and replace. Poly pipe can also be pinched by kinks along its length or by stones or rocks pressing into it. If so, part of the circuit will fail to operate. Dig up the circuit, starting from the last fully functioning spray head or emitter, and straighten the kink or remove the obstruction. The pipe should be buried in sand to prevent further blockage. Test the circuit before covering the pipe again.

CORRECTING VALVE PROBLEMS: Modern valves are less subject to sticking than older ones and are much easier to adjust. Problems with excess or insufficient flow (see page 93) are easily corrected by adjusting the

REPAIRING PVC PIPE WITH A REPAIR COUPLING

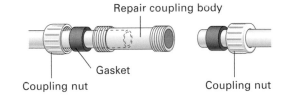

Repair coupling body

Gasket

Coupling nut

Coupling nut

REPAIRING PVC PIPE BY REPLACING DAMAGED SECTION

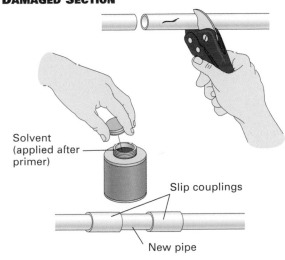

Solvent (applied after primer)

Slip couplings

New pipe

REPAIRING THE SYSTEM
continued

WIPER SEAL MAINTENANCE

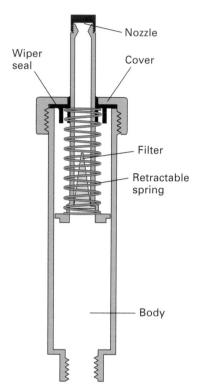

flow control. Each model has a different type of control, but most are easily adjusted by hand with a wrench or a special key. Leave the circuit running as you turn the flow control so you can check results.

You may need a helper to report on the results if the spray head is not visible from the control valve.

When a circuit doesn't shut off automatically or when it won't open, there may be a problem with a control valve. If so, try opening and closing the valve rapidly while the water is running to dislodge any dirt. If that fails, turn off the water and take the valve apart according to the manufacturer's instructions, removing any debris or buildup, and looking for cracks or other damage. Often the problem is an overly tightened flow control. Before reinstalling the valve stem, lubricate it according to the manufacturer's instructions. Cracked or damaged control valves can sometimes be repaired, but are best replaced with new ones.

SPRAY HEAD MAINTENANCE

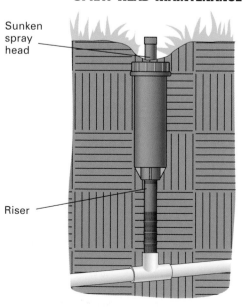

When a manual control valve is hard to turn or sticks, see if the threads on the valve stem have been damaged (this can happen if the valve stem was improperly installed). If so, replace the valve stem. If the threads on the valve itself are damaged, it will need to be replaced. If none of the circuits operates, check the main control valve. You may simply have forgotten to turn it on after the system was closed down for the winter. Or it could be faulty and require cleaning or replacement, as explained above. Automatic valves not opening or closing properly may also be due to a damaged controller.

DIAGNOSING CONTROLLER PROBLEMS:

Automatic irrigation systems which depend on the efficient operation of the controller are subject to a number of problems, most due to faulty wiring. When the circuit breaker controlling an automatic irrigation system trips or when valves fail to open or close, even though the valves have been thoroughly cleaned and inspected, the cause is generally a poor wire connection or a shorted wire. Make sure the circuit breaker is off and check all wire connections, including those at the automatic controller, circuit valves, and main valve. Repair any that look faulty. Make sure the connections are properly sealed and waterproofed. Water in contact with a bare wire is a common cause of malfunction. If the connections seem intact, you may have to dig up part of the inoperative circuit to trace the location of a break in the wire.

PREVENTING SPRAY HEAD AND EMITTER PROBLEMS

Careful and regular cleaning (see page 88) will prevent most spray head and emitter problems. Make sure that nozzles and emitters are washed; that filters are cleaned and, if necessary, replaced; and that the circuit is flushed regularly. Pop-up spray heads present special problems. If they refuse to pop up or retract, the problem is usually the wiper seal, a rubber or plastic gasket designed to keep dirt out of the spray head. Remove the nozzle (see the manufacturer's instructions) and clean it. If the wiper seal appears worn or torn, replace it. In older pop-up heads especially, springs tend to rust and may need to be replaced.

Soil often builds up over the years, especially in lawns, obstructing heads more and more until they no longer irrigate efficiently. When buildup occurs, simply dig around the head, down to the main pipe, flush thoroughly, then turn off the circuit and replace the riser with a taller one. Flush again before you reinstall the spray head. If you chose adjustable risers to start with, they can be adjusted to the new height by twisting.

PROBLEM SOLVING

Malfunctions in irrigation systems aren't common, and most that do occur are straightforward and easy to correct, such as worn-out gaskets and partly plugged nozzles. This chart will help you solve most irrigation system problems.

Symptom	Check for	Action
Flow reduced	Clogged filter	Clean and rinse filter
	Flow control poorly adjusted	Adjust flow control at circuit control valve
	Sediment buildup	Flush system
Circuit won't shut off automatically	Dirt or sediments in valve	Open and close valve rapidly to dislodge sediments. If that fails, remove valve cap and blow out unit with compressed air
	Faulty valve	Overhaul or replace valve
Circuit breaker tripped	Faulty automatic valve	Replace valve
	Poor or shorted wire connection	Verify and waterproof connections or replace wire
Pop-up sprayer won't pop up	Screen or filter basket clogged	Clean and rinse filter
	Debris in wiper seal	Remove nozzle and clean wiper seal
Pop-up sprayer won't retract	Debris in wiper seal	Remove nozzle and clean wiper seal
	Wiper seal torn	Remove nozzle and replace wiper seal
	Rusty spring in spray head	Replace spring
Spray doesn't break up into fine water droplets	Pressure too low	Run circuit when no other water being used. Reduce number of outlets on circuit
Distortion of spray pattern	Reduced flow	Adjust flow control at circuit control valve
Valve doesn't irrigate	Faulty valve	Overhaul or replace valve
	Shutoff valve or other valve closed	Check system and open valve
	Common wire in controller not connected	Reconnect common wire
	Poor wire connection	Verify wire connection
	Break in wire	Repair or replace wire
	Valve flow stem tightened too far	Loosen valve flow stem
Spray pattern incomplete	Dirt or debris in nozzle	Clean nozzle
Spray head below soil level	Soil has built up over years	Replace riser with taller one
		Twist adjustable riser upward
Rotary sprayer splashes excessively	Lack of splash guard	Add splash guard
Water puddles	Leak in system	Locate leak, and plug or replace part
	Punctured drip line	Use hole plug to repair leak
	Overly long irrigation period	Irrigate for shorter period of time
Excess runoff	Overly long irrigation period	Irrigate for shorter period of time
	Slope of yard too steep	Irrigate slopes for shorter periods but more often
	Slope of yard too steep	Adjust rate of spray
Manual valve stuck or hard to turn	Dirt in valve	Clean and lubricate valve
	Threads damaged	Replace valve stem and lubricate
Water backs up into house	No backflow prevention	Install backflow prevention
No water reaching part of circuit	Kink in supply pipe	Remove kink
	Rock pressing on supply pipe	Remove rock and surround pipe with sand
	Buildup of debris and sediments	Flush out sector
Emitter not functioning	Emitter clogged	Clean or replace emitter
Part of circuit too dry	Not enough emitters	Add emitters or replace emitters with higher-gallonage ones
Part of circuit too moist	Too many emitters	Remove some emitters and plug pipe or replace emitters with lower-gallonage ones
Emitters come loose	Excess pressure	Add pressure regulation device
Containers too dry	Not enough irrigation	Add more emitters. Put containers on separate circuit to allow for more frequent irrigation
Containers too wet	Too much irrigation	Remove emitters. Put containers on separate circuit to allow for frequent but short periods of irrigation
Pipes damaged during winter	System improperly drained	Drain system each fall in cold climates. Add drainage valves at lowest point in each circuit. Verify and repair damages
	Poly pipe too stretched	Add additional length of pipe

INDEX

Boldface numbers indicate pages with photographs or illustrations related to the topic.

METRIC CONVERSIONS

U.S. Units to Metric Equivalents			Metric Units to U.S. Equivalents		
To Convert From	Multiply By	To Get	To Convert From	Multiply By	To Get
Inches	25.4	Millimetres	Millimetres	0.0394	Inches
Inches	2.54	Centimetres	Centimetres	0.3937	Inches
Feet	30.48	Centimetres	Centimetres	0.0328	Feet
Feet	0.3048	Metres	Metres	3.2808	Feet
Yards	0.9144	Metres	Metres	1.0936	Yards
Square inches	6.4516	Square centimetres	Square centimetres	0.1550	Square inches
Square feet	0.0929	Square metres	Square metres	10.764	Square feet
Square yards	0.8361	Square metres	Square metres	1.1960	Square yards
Acres	0.4047	Hectares	Hectares	2.4711	Acres
Cubic inches	16.387	Cubic centimetres	Cubic centimetres	0.0610	Cubic inches
Cubic feet	0.0283	Cubic metres	Cubic metres	35.315	Cubic feet
Cubic feet	28.316	Litres	Litres	0.0353	Cubic feet
Cubic yards	0.7646	Cubic metres	Cubic metres	1.308U	Cubic yards
Cubic yards	764.55	Litres	Litres	0.0013	Cubic yards

To convert from degrees Fahrenheit (F) to degrees Celsius (C), first subtract 32, then multiply by 5/9.

To convert from degrees Celsius to degrees Fahrenheit, multiply by 9/5, then add 32.